The Strange Case of Dr. Jekyll & Mr Hyde -- A Study Guide

Francis Gilbert &

Robert Louis Stevenson

ABOUT THE AUTHOR

Francis Gilbert is a writer who has been a secondary school
teacher for over twenty years in various state schools. He has
published numerous books, including *I'm A Teacher, Get Me Out
Of Here* and *The Last Day of Term* as well as a series of study
guides on classic texts such William Blake's *Songs of Innocence
and Experience*, *Frankenstein*, *Wuthering Heights* and *Jane Eyre*
-- all published on Kindle. For more: www.francisgilbert.co.uk

DEDICATION

To all my GCSE classes, especially the ones who have studied
Stevenson's mysterious novel with me.

ACKNOWLEDGMENTS

Thanks, as ever, to Erica Wagner for helping me with my writing &
all the teachers who have supported me over the years.

Contents

1 Contexts

Understanding Contexts

In order to fully appreciate a text, you need to understand the context, or background, in which it was written – known as its contexts of writing – and the contexts in which you read the book, or the contexts of reading. This is potentially a huge area to explore because 'contexts' essentially mean the 'worlds' from which the book has arisen and the worlds it creates in the reader's mind. For the best books, these are many and various. The most obvious starting point is the writer's own life: it is worth thinking about how and why the events in a writer's life might have influenced his or her fiction. However, you do have to be careful not to assume too much. For example, you must remember that Dr Jekyll, while he might have been based upon some real people that Robert Louis Stevenson knew in his life, is a character in his own right in the novel – a vital cog in the narrative wheel, a literary construct and not a real person.

It is particularly fruitful to explore other contexts of writing. We can look at the broader world from which Stevenson arose (Victorian society and the values that it promoted), and consider carefully how, in his writing, he both adopted and rejected the morals of his time. Other contexts might be the influence of the literary world that Stevenson inhabited (what other authors were writing at the time), how religion shaped his views, and so on.

Just as important as the contexts of *writing* are the contexts of *reading*: how we read the novel today. Most of us before we read *The Strange Case of Dr Jekyll and Mr Hyde* will actually know the outcome of the story and many of the major incidents; this will affect the way we read it profoundly, particularly if we have seen one of the many filmed versions. Your own personal context is very important too. If you have particular views about human nature, you may find the novel even more interesting. If, for example, you feel that human beings may have two sides to their nature, a good and evil side, then you may feel more engaged with the novel. In order for you to fully consider the contexts of reading rather than my telling you what to think, I have posed open-ended questions that get you thinking about your own views.

Contexts of Writing: Stevenson's Life

You can watch a YouTube video about Stevenson's life here:
http://www.youtube.com/watch?v=yRxC5ETN8Zc

Stevenson was born in 1850: the middle of the nineteenth century. He is a figure who straddles both the Victorian and the modern age: his writing appears Victorian on the surface, in its language, settings and characters, but dig deeper and you find a modern interest in the darker sides of the human mind.

Growing up in Edinburgh, the son of an engineer and a religious mother, he suffered numerous illnesses as a child which were tended to by his fundamentalist Christian nurse, Alison Cunningham or 'Cummy'. Both his nurse and his parents instilled in him a strong sense of good and evil, talking to him at length about the consequences of sin, which was to perish eternally in the flames of Hell on Judgment Day. Cummy's talk of Hell gave the young Stevenson nightmares that were to plague him for the rest of his life. Most significantly, Stevenson saw humans as essentially "dualistic" creatures, split personalities who were both good and evil in equal measure.

This dualism was reflected in the world that Stevenson inhabited. Edinburgh had both an 'Old' and 'New Town'. Being from a rich family, Stevenson lived in the pleasant, wide streets of the New Town, but was aware of the filthy, disgusting over-crowded conditions of the Old Town. As he grew older, he came to realise that the New Town derived its wealth in part from the labourers who lived in the Old Town: Stevenson worked out that the two worlds were reliant upon each other.

Moreover, Edinburgh also had a dark past, which Stevenson was fascinated by. There were stories of William 'Deacon' Brodie who appeared to be an upright craftsman by day, but was a criminal at night until he was hanged in 1788. As a teenager, Stevenson worked upon a script based on Brodie's life. Stevenson also knew about Burke and Hare, who in the 1820s, would murder people in order to supply Edinburgh Medical College with bodies to experiment upon. The respectable Dr. Knox was their main customer.

Stevenson himself led something of a double life. While a student studying engineering at Edinburgh University, he would spend a great deal of time in the dives of the Old Town, drinking and probably sleeping with prostitutes. He left Edinburgh in 1873, and travelled abroad. This was the real beginning of his literary career. After suffering from a physical collapse, he travelled widely and frequently in France: the warmer climate suited him better than the cold of Scotland. In France, he made many trips to the Forest of Fontainebleau, staying at Barbizon, Grez-sur-Loing and Nemours, visiting art galleries and joining artists' communities there. He also made the journeys described most famously in his travel book, *Travels with a Donkey in the Cévennes*. Although his parents thought he was wasting his time, he was developing a powerful voice as a writer.

While in Grez, France, he met Fanny Osbourne: she was married with two children but this did not stop him from falling in love with her. A year later, he met her again and spent much of his time with her and her children. Fanny returned to American and began divorce proceedings in San Francisco. Desperate to see her again, against the wishes of his friends and parents, Stevenson embarked upon the long journey to join her, sailing to New York, and then taking the train to California.

After many adventures, including a total breakdown of his health, he arrived in San Francisco, where he married Fanny. Later the couple returned to Scotland, where he wrote in collaboration with W.E. Henley, *Deacon Brodie*, his first play. In 1882, he moved to France, publishing *Treasure Island* in 1883. However with his health getting worse, he returned to England and settled in Bournemouth, which remained his home until 1887. Thus began the most productive and successful period of his writing career. Despite being gravely ill, he wrote and published, *A Child's Garden of Verses*, *Dr Jekyll and Mr Hyde* and *Kidnapped* during this time. The death of his father in 1887, Thomas Stevenson, prompted Stevenson to look again for a warm climate to live in. He visited the South Seas. He chartered a yacht and spent three years sailing around the eastern and central Pacific, visiting important island groups and stopping off for extended stays in Hawaii, getting to know the local royalty and railing against the stupidity and arrogance of the missionaries. In 1890, he settled with his family on one of the Samoan islands, becoming known as Tusitala, or "story-writer" in Samoan. Once again, he came into conflict with the Europeans on the island, feeling that the colonists were running the island in a corrupt and incompetent fashion. After suffering from depression, he resumed writing, but died suddenly of a cerebral hemorrhage in 1894, at the age of 44.

His writing of *Dr Jekyll and Mr Hyde* is now, like the writing of *Frankenstein*, the stuff of legend. He wrote it in 1885 while living in Bournemouth, publishing it in 1886. Mrs Stevenson recounted:

> In the small hours of one morning, I was awakened by cries of horror from Louis. Thinking he had a nightmare, I woke him. He said angrily, 'Why did you wake me? I was dreaming a fine bogey tale.' I had awakened him at the first transformation scene. He had had in his mind an idea of a double life story, but it was not the same as the dream. He asked me, as usual, to make no criticisms until the first draft was done...In this tale I felt and still feel he was hampered by his dream. The powder – which I thought might be changed – he couldn't eliminate because he saw it so plainly in the dream. In the original story he had Jekyll bad all through, and working for the Hyde change only for a disguise. I didn't like the opening, which was confused – again the dream – and proposed that Hyde should run over the child showing that he was an evil force without humanity. After quite a long interval his bell rang for me, and ...I went upstairs. As I entered the door Louis pointed with a long dramatic finger (you know) to a pile of ashes on the hearth of the fireplace saying that I was right and there was the tale. I nearly fainted away with misery and horror when I saw all was gone. He was already hard at work at the new version which was finished in a few days more.

There is some debate as to exactly how the story was written, with some critics agreeing that Mrs Stevenson played a pivotal role in shaping the story, but others disagreeing. No one will know for sure. But whatever the exact history of the writing of the story, the drafting process was intensive but furiously quick. Lloyd Osbourne, Stevenson's stepson, said: "I don't believe that there was ever such a literary feat before as the writing of *Dr Jekyll*. I remember the first reading as if it were yesterday. Louis came downstairs in a fever; read nearly half the book aloud; and then, while we were still gasping, he was away again, and busy writing. I doubt if the first draft took so long as three days". Having listened to his wife's criticisms and thought about the story further Stevenson re-wrote the story again in three to six days. He then re-wrote the story again over the space of four to six weeks. In truth, although written quickly, the story was the product of a life-time interest in dreams, the Gothic genre, and the fundamental duality of man. The story was more or less an immediate bestseller, with forty thousand copies being sold in six months. By 1901, it was estimated to have sold over 250,000 copies -- a huge number for a book of that time. Critics of the day generally received the story favourably. One reviewer was quick to perceive that Stevenson's narrative was truly original in one respect. When talking about Edward Hyde, the critic said:

> with its unlikeness to its master, with its hideous caprices, and appalling vitality, and terrible power of growth and increase, is, to our thinking, a notion as novel as it is terrific. We would welcome a spectre, a ghoul, or even a vampire gladly, rather than meet Mr Edward Hyde.

Questions

Why was Stevenson's religious upbringing influential in shaping the themes of *Dr Jekyll and Mr Hyde*?

How did growing up in Edinburgh influence the writing of *Dr Jekyll*?

In what ways was Stevenson's behaviour in his life similar to that of Dr Jekyll? In what ways was it different?

How did Stevenson make his living from writing?

How did *Dr Jekyll and Mr Hyde* come to be written? Who was influential in the re-drafting of the manuscript?

How successful was the novel? Why was it successful do you think?

POSSIBLE ANSWERS in brief & bold

Why was Stevenson's religious upbringing influential in shaping the themes of *Dr Jekyll and Mr Hyde*? **Although Stevenson became an atheist later on in life, he was profoundly affected by the tales he heard about sinners being punished for their sins in hell, and the ways in which religion made people feel shame about sex and desire. *Dr Jekyll* is full of religious references to the Devil and to behaviour which religion deemed sinful. Jekyll pretends to be religious and pious but desperately wants to be sinful. Stevenson's religious upbringing – including his nanny's "hellfire" stories – affected him deeply.**

How did growing up in Edinburgh influence the writing of *Dr Jekyll*? **Although *Dr Jekyll* is set in London, many critics think Stevenson is describing the Edinburgh of his childhood where there was an "Old Town", which was run-down and poverty-stricken like the place where Hyde lives, and a "New Town" which was posh and rich, like Jekyll's house. This "dualism" –**

having two sides – was the central theme of the book: how a city and people themselves have a good and an evil side.

In what ways was Stevenson's behaviour in his life similar to that of Dr Jekyll? In what ways was it different? **Stevenson probably led a "secret" life as a student: he probably visited prostitutes, and took drugs such as alcohol. He also took the painkiller opium to help him with his illnesses: this drug-taking is similar to Jekyll's drug-taking. However, Stevenson did not feel the desire to appear respectable in the way that Jekyll does: he led a Bohemian life that was very different from most middle-class people of his day.**

How did Stevenson make his living from writing? **He wrote many different types of texts: he found success as a children's writer but was also a poet, critic, essayist and adult novelist, as we see with *Dr Jekyll*.**

How did *Dr Jekyll and Mr Hyde* come to be written? Who was influential in the re-drafting of the manuscript? **The novel was the result of a nightmare Stevenson had where he dreamt about a man having a double which haunted him. His wife made him re-write the novel because she felt that it didn't have a clear moral or point.**

How successful was the novel? Why was it successful do you think? **The novel was tremendously successful, by far the most successful book Stevenson wrote, and sold a quarter of a million copies in Stevenson's life-time, a huge number for a novel of its day. It explored the nightmares of the Victorian middle-class in the form of a thrilling, "sensational" story: it showed how supposedly respectable people were, in fact, evil.**

Selected Reading on Stevenson's Life

One of the best places to start learning about Stevenson is the Robert Louis Stevenson website:

http://www.robert-louis-stevenson.org/

The Wikipedia entry on Stevenson is useful: http://en.wikipedia.org/wiki/Robert_Louis_Stevenson

Clare Harman: *Robert Louis Stevenson – A Biography* (Harper Perennial; 2006) A landmark book on Stevenson, brilliantly researched.

G.K. Chesterton: *Robert Louis Stevenson* (House of Stratus; 2001)

Chesterton's biography written in the early 20th century is a concise classic.

Contexts of Reading

We read the story of *Jekyll and Hyde* very differently now. For us, the story is less about a battle between good and evil and more about one man's battles with his repressed nature. Above all, it seems to us now that the novel is about 'repression'. It is clear from the text that Dr Henry Jekyll is a deeply repressed man: a man who wishes to appear very respectable to the outside world and yet deep down harbours many secret desires that he is not able to pursue openly. Thus the transformation into Hyde becomes a wonderful 'disguise'.

While we are a more open society now, many powerful people are still "Jekyll and Hyde" characters. It is clear that important people in the media, politics and education have to put on a respectable facade in order to further their careers, and yet harbour secret desires that they would not want anyone to know about. The most spectacular case of this is the story of Bill Clinton's presidency, which was ruined by what has come to be known as the 'Monica Lewinsky' scandal. Clinton had an affair with a young intern in the White House and attempted to cover it up: the 'cover up' nearly led to him being impeached for lying to the American people about the truth of the affair. Obviously, people like Clinton would benefit greatly if they had had a potion like Henry Jekyll's!

Many critics have also begun to view the narrative as an allegory about addiction. One of the central issues of the notion is Jekyll's addiction to taking the potion and to being "transformed" into another person. Towards the end of the novel, it is clear that Jekyll can't wean himself off the drug. As a result, like a junkie, his whole physical and mental condition deteriorates. The last section of the book could be viewed as a horrific description of the nightmare of addiction: his ransacking the town for the drug, his violent mood swings, his wish to hide away from everyone. In such a way, we could say that the novel has become more relevant than ever because it tackles issues which are problems in our society.

Questions

Why is the novel about repression?
Why has the novel become so influential in popular and literary culture?
What issues does the novel raise that are still in our minds today?

POSSIBLE ANSWERS in brief & bold

Why is the novel about repression? **Dr Jekyll buries and hides his secret desires and wishes, and this repression leads to him developing a "Hyde" character who is a way of finding an outlet for these desires.**

Why has the novel become so influential in popular and literary culture? **Stevenson revealed something which is prevalent in modern culture: he showed that people in power, who are respectable, often have secret, inner lives which can come to dominate them at the expense of their careers, e.g. President Clinton.**

What issues does the novel raise that are still in our minds today? **Apart from its focus upon repression, the novel explores the consequences of drug addiction and possibly madness.**

2 Structure

How Stevenson shapes his narrative around certain themes

> You can watch a YouTube video I made about the plot of the book, entitled 'Learn the Plot of Dr Jekyll in Five Minutes' here:
> http://www.youtube.com/watch?v=zV3QxszjtPE

The novel has a complex structure because it has several different narrators. This is largely because Stevenson wishes to make the story a mystery story with the central issue being: who is Edward Hyde and what is his connection to Henry Jekyll? In order to construct a mystery story, Stevenson could not have Jekyll narrating until the very end of the book when the mystery has been solved. In this sense, the novel is a proto-type detective novel. The lawyer Utterson plays the role of the detective, narrating more or less continuously, the first three sections of the book. The fourth section is Lanyon's narrative, which at the end reveals that Jekyll is Hyde, and then the final section is Jekyll's narrative, which tells us, with the mystery solved, how he became Hyde.

As has been already noted, the novel is structured around the theme of repression. Most of the novel's most striking images are connected in one form or another around the idea of repression. The locked doors and curtained windows of Jekyll's house are images of a man locking away the truth that lurks inside; the image of Jekyll turning into Hyde could possibly be a metaphor of what happens when the unconscious mind is revealed; the murder of Carew is possibly a symbol of the repressed mind striking out at the conscious one. The narrative is about the unpeeling of the layers that hide the repressed desires inside Jekyll. We could break down the novel into the following structure:

Opening (Section 1: Story Of The Door, Search for Mr Hyde, Dr Jekyll was quite at ease)
This is Utterson's narrative, in which he tells us about his cousin witnessing a brutal assault upon an eight-year-old
-      Suspecting that Jekyll is involved with this terrible character, Utterson spies upon Hyde and meets him. He believes that Jekyll is being blackmailed by Hyde.
-      We meet the slick, superficial Dr. Lanyon and hear about Jekyll's strange experiments.

Complications (Section 2: The Carew Murder Case)
-      London is shocked by the murder of Danvers Carew, a respectable MP. Hyde is suspected. His flat is raided but he is not found.
-      When Utterson visits Jekyll, he finds him sick and depressed. He suspects that Jekyll has forged a letter to protect Hyde.

Crisis (Section 3: Remarkable Incident Of Dr Lanyon)
-      Hyde has vanished. Jekyll joins society, socialising widely. For two months, Jekyll is once again respectable man, but then returns to seclusion.
-      The pompous Lanyon is also much changed, apparently mortally ill and wanting nothing to do with Jekyll.
-      Lanyon dies. He has written a letter which is not to be opened until Jekyll dies or disappears.
-      Jekyll continues to decline. A strange man is spotted in his house. At the request of Jekyll's servant, Poole, Utterson breaks into Jekyll's laboratory and finds Hyde lying dead, dwarfed by Jekyll's larger clothes.

Climax (Section 4: Dr Lanyon's narrative)
-      Utterson reads Lanyon's account in which he learns that Lanyon was asked to find some powders for Jekyll.
-      Hyde arrives at Lanyon's house, mixes a potion and becomes Jekyll before Lanyon's eyes.

Resolution (Section 5: Henry Jekyll's Statement Of The Case)

-   Jekyll tells his story, talking about his essential dual nature, his search for a potion which enable him to become someone else, his transformation into Hyde
-   He explains how Hyde begins to take over. He can no longer control his transformations. Jekyll has become utterly corrupted.

Questions

What themes does Stevenson explore in the novel?

How and why does he structure the novel around these themes?

POSSIBLE ANSWERS in brief & bold

What themes does Stevenson explore in the novel? **Stevenson explores the theme of repression in the novel and the ways in which people repress their inner-most desires and hide their secret wishes.**

How and why does he structure the novel around these themes?

The novel is structured around the themes of repression and dualism because it slowly reveals Jekyll's inner life and desires as the mystery is unraveled. Hyde is Jekyll's inner-most repressed desires and this is why he is so destructive.

3 Genre

The blending of science fiction, the gothic and the detective genres

The most influential genre upon this work is the Gothic. Stevenson's descriptions of the smoggy London streets, his vivid imagery when describing the horrible Mr Hyde, the mysterious narrative with its kernel of horror at the heart of it are all elements which you might find in a Gothic story. The Gothic emerged as a very popular form of entertainment in the 18th century with writers like Horace Walpole and Mrs Radcliffe writing novels about nasty aristocrats living in haunted castles and attempting to seduce innocent damsels in distress. The novels were extremely successful because they combined haunted settings with racy narratives that were about beautiful girls being pursued by unscrupulous men.

The Gothic influenced Mary Shelley when she wrote the first science fiction novel, *Frankenstein*, in 1818. The impact of Mary Shelley's novel *Frankenstein* cannot be underestimated in terms of its influence upon Stevenson's novella, *Dr Jekyll and Mr Hyde*. In many ways, Shelley set the template which all other science fiction narratives have imitated since: an obsessive scientist who pays the consequences for his meddling with the structure of the human body and brain. Stevenson's fiction contains a similar 'Promethean' figure to Mary Shelley's Victor Frankenstein. Henry Jekyll is like the Greek hero Prometheus who brought fire to mankind – he offers man the chance to become another person entirely with his potion. Like Victor Frankenstein, he creates a 'new being' in the form of Hyde.

Another Gothic story which influenced Stevenson is Edgar Allen Poe's story about a man who has a double called 'William Wilson'. There are also strong correlations to James Hogg's *Private Memoirs and Confessions of a Justified Sinner*. Stevenson's narrative has many similarities with Hogg's in that it has overlapping third and first person narratives, and contains a man who is motivated to murder by a strange, ghost-like demonic alter ego.

However, Stevenson's novel takes the Gothic one stage further than all of these novels by being more 'concentrated' and, in some ways, more simple. Stevenson intensifies the horror in his novel by concentrating upon the character of Hyde and not introducing lots of peripheral characters. The novel is more psychological than any other previous efforts in that it makes it clear that it is Jekyll's psychology which creates Hyde: that Hyde is a manifestation of Jekyll's character. More than other writers, Stevenson takes the time to establish a memorable setting, evoking the foggy London streets, the locked doors, the mysterious laboratories in intense detail. He is a much more technically accomplished writer than Mary Shelley: he does not need to pile event upon horrific event to create the horror in the book. He is able to build suspense by evoking character and setting.

Most significantly, Stevenson creates many of the trademark features of the science fiction and detective genres here. His descriptions of the making of the potion and the transformation of Jekyll into Hyde are masterful set-pieces which have been imitated so much since that it is difficult now to appreciate their power when they were first written. Likewise, Utterson's uncovering of the mystery has now become the template for most detective stories: his spying on his suspects, his investigations into the relevant documents, his interviews with various characters from different social settings are all the stock-in-trade of the detective story now.

Thus we can see that the novel is a brilliantly successful blend of genres: the Gothic, the science fiction narrative, and the detective story.

Key ways in which Dr Jekyll conforms to the Gothic genre:

Its focus upon a horrible **villain**;

Description of **horrific incidents**: the death of Carew and Hyde;

The **atmosphere** is ghostly and spooky with lots of darkness and fog;

There are **innocent victims**: a girl of eight, Danvers Carew, and possibly Henry Jekyll – who is both guilty and innocent?

Ways in which it doesn't conform:

The **structure** of the story: the narrative operates like a detective novel in that we have one character, Utterson, searching for the solution to the mystery;

The **urban setting**: most Gothic novels are set in castles or the remote countryside. Stevenson invented an entirely new genre, the "urban gothic", which was later imitated by Sir Arthur Conan-Doyle in his Sherlock Holmes stories and many films such as *Seven*;

The **psychology** of the characters: all the characters in the novel are psychologically convincing, they are not stereotypical heroes and villains;

The lack of any **hero**: the closest the story gets to a hero is Utterson, who fails to save his friend but does, like a detective, uncover the mystery;

The **solution** to the mystery. There had been many Gothic stories with doppelgangers (doubles) in which the hero was hunted by a double or alter ego, someone who looks very like him but behaves in an evil fashion. But no story until this one had the "double" – in this case Mr Hyde – being the same as the main protagonist, Dr Jekyll.

Questions

In what ways does the story operate like a detective novel?
In what ways does it contain elements of the Gothic novel?
In what ways is the novel different from many Gothic novels?

POSSIBLE ANSWERS in brief & bold

In what ways does the story operate like a detective novel? **Mr Utterson is like a detective in the novel, slowly unearthing and discovering the truth about Dr Jekyll and Mr Hyde, finding clues about Hyde's violence and misdemeanours, and interviewing people, reading documents and breaking down doors to discover the truth about Jekyll.**
In what ways does it contain elements of the Gothic novel? **The foggy atmosphere, the monstrous Hyde, the violence and the extreme emotions expressed are all Gothic in atmosphere.**
In what ways is the novel different from many Gothic novels? **The lack of any hero and the solution to the mystery are not typically Gothic in that when we discover Hyde is Jekyll the whole novel becomes psychological.**

4 Critical Perspectives

Is this novel about the unconscious?

Dreams played a central role in the writing of the story and form an important part of the narrative. His wife's view of the dream being a distraction from writing the story was not an opinion shared by Stevenson himself, who, in an interview, said:

> At night I dreamed the story, not precisely as it is written, for of course there are always stupidities in dreams, but practically it came to me as a gift...Even when fast asleep I know that it is I who am inventing, and when I cry out it is with gratification to know that the story is so good...For instance, all I dreamed about Dr Jekyll was that one man was being pressed into a cabinet, when he swallowed a drug and changed into another being...

Here we can see how it was Stevenson's 'unconscious' mind – the part of the mind that is expressed in dreams – which helped shape the narrative.

Stevenson was writing at a time when many philosophers and scientists were beginning to examine the role of dreams and the unconscious in influencing human behaviour. Stevenson wrote the book at a time when people's interest in the 'unconscious' – which is supposed to influence our actions without us knowing it – was growing. In 1885, the French neurologist Charcot had given a public display of hypnotism in Paris. The great French scientist used hypnosis to induce a state of hysteria in patients and studied the results, and was single-handedly responsible for changing the medical community's perception of hypnosis: previously they'd thought of it as 'mesmerism', effectively no better than supernatural hokum. But Charcot showed how there were powerful 'unconscious forces' at work in shaping what people do, particularly in hysterics and neurotics.

Perhaps even more relevant to an understanding of *Jekyll and Hyde* is an appreciation of the work of Krafft-Ebing and Freud. While it is unlikely that Stevenson had heard of either, there is no doubt that the ideas that they explored and theorised about interested Stevenson. It's clear that there was a 'zeitgeist' at this time: a coming together of ideas, art and science. Many of the top writers, thinkers and scientists were fascinated by the realm of the 'unconscious'. Krafft-Ebing's *Psychopathia Sexualis* was published in 1886. For the first time, Krafft-Ebing's work charted the different sorts of sexual desire, male and female, homosexual and heterosexual. While many of his views now would be regarded as offensive, at the time they were very progressive. Fundamentally, he began to uncover the role of sexuality in society, showing that these hidden desires are often battling with the conventional moral standards of the day. Thus, like Stevenson, he suggests that man is a 'dualistic' creature, appearing respectable and pleasant, but deep down suffering from frustrated, repressed desires. Sigmund Freud took these ideas a step further and proposed that sexual desire was the main motivation in life.

In his book, *The Interpretation of Dreams* (1899), Freud explored this notion in some depth. He called dreams the "royal road to the unconscious". This meant that dreams can tell us about the language of the unconscious. In particular, they can tell us about the desires we "repress" in our life. In such a way, Freud would interpret certain objects in dreams as being sexual symbols: apertures of any sort could be metaphors for the vagina, while protruding objects could represent the erect penis, being what Freud calls a 'phallic symbol'. Freud argued that the human mind was divided into three main components: the 'Super-Ego', which is the part of the mind which "controls" you and makes you behave, the "Id" which is the part that expresses pure desire, such as sexual desire, while the 'Ego' tries to mediate or deal with the differing demands of the Id and the Super-Ego.

While many of his ideas were clearly not known by Stevenson, there is no doubt that Hyde is an intensely sexual creature, playing out his sexual fantasies in the smoggy streets of London: he is in many ways a literary embodiment of Freud's 'Id'. It could be argued indeed that Hyde is a metaphor for the 'unconscious' of man: he is the ape-like creature that we would all rather hide from civilised society. While our unconscious might want to punch people who annoy us, our civilised side prevents us from doing so. While we might want to have sex much more frequently than we do, our desire to appear respectable and not "randy" stops us from propositioning every person we fancy. It is clear that Hyde suffers from no such inhibitions. Thus, there is a powerful argument that the novel is very disturbing still because Hyde represents the unconscious in all of us.

Questions

What might be a "Freudian" reading of the novel?

Why could you argue that the novel is actually about the "unconscious"?

POSSIBLE ANSWERS in brief & bold

What might be a "Freudian" reading of the novel? **One could see Hyde as an expression of Freud's the "Id": he is pure desire unchecked by the Ego or the Super-Ego, desire let off the leash, able to do exactly what it wants. Meanwhile, Dr Jekyll has a "Super-Ego", a controlling, moralizing part of his mind, but it grows weaker as Hyde, the "Id" becomes stronger. In the middle, the real Jekyll, the "Ego" becomes hopelessly lost trying to deal with the competing demands of the Id and the Super-Ego.**

Why could you argue that the novel is actually about the "unconscious"? **Hyde might be an expression of the unconscious desires of mankind: what men really want to do if they weren't "hemmed in" by modern society's rules and regulations.**

Selected Reading

Norton Critical Editions: *The Strange Case of Dr Jekyll and Mr Hyde* (Norton: 2003) This is by far and away the best "academic" edition of the book, packed with great critical essays as well as comprehensive notes: it is aimed at undergraduates studying the book at university.

David Daiches: *Robert Louis Stevenson and His World* (Pictorial Biography: 1973) Although this is an old book, it remains the best for evoking the world that Stevenson lived in and has an excellent section of Jekyll and Hyde.

5 Use of language

A writer's first and only tool is language. Writers create settings, characters, and stories out of language. This is no mean feat: unlike film-makers they don't have moving images, sound, and music to create atmosphere, believable people and engaging narratives. Stevenson's audience would have been highly educated but the vast majority of people in his day were not literate: they could not read and write – and obviously could not read his books. They were expected to be servants, factory-workers and assistants in shops. However, there was a growing group of people called the middle class who had been well-educated and were highly literate. In the days before cinema, television, the internet, one of the main forms of entertainment for wealthy, educated people was reading stories in magazines and novels. Many well-off families would read to each other in the evenings and avidly bought the latest fashionable book. As a result, some writers could make a living by selling their fiction to this eager audience.

Until *Jekyll and Hyde*, Stevenson had struggled to make money, but this novel was to change everything. It was sensationally popular. In terms of style, it was written like many novels of the day: in a highly literary, ornate style in places, but in a more simple style in others. We may find this difficult to understand but educated readers took delight in reading complex sentences and sophisticated vocabulary: it was a "badge of honour" to know difficult words. However, the writing couldn't be too difficult as to be unreadable. Stevenson strikes a balance in *Jekyll and Hyde*: some parts – particularly when Jekyll explains his psychology – are very complicated, but others are fairly simple to understand, particularly the dialogue.

In some of the most dramatic parts of the novel, Stevenson thinks and writes like a playwright. Hyde does not speak very much but when he does the effect is electrifying and suspenseful. Let's look at this interaction between Hyde and Utterson in Chapter 2, *The Search for Mr Hyde*:

> "Yes," returned Mr. Hyde, "It is as well we have met; and apropos, you should have my address." And he gave a number of a street in Soho.

"Good God!" thought Mr. Utterson, "can he, too, have been thinking of the will?" But he kept his feelings to himself and only grunted in acknowledgment of the address.

"And now," said the other, "how did you know me?"

"By description," was the reply.

"Whose description?"

"We have common friends," said Mr. Utterson.

"Common friends," echoed Mr. Hyde, a little hoarsely. "Who are they?"

"Jekyll, for instance," said the lawyer.

"He never told you," cried Mr. Hyde, with a flush of anger. "I did not think you would have lied."

Notice in the dialogue how Stevenson generates a powerful "subtext": what matters is what is not said. We see this very vividly in Hyde's first comment about how it is good that he has met Utterson because Utterson needs to know where he lives. Utterson realises that this is because Hyde is aware that he is in the will and Utterson, being Jekyll's lawyer, will need to contact him if Jekyll dies or disappears and give him all of Jekyll's money. Thus we can see that a simple comment is laced with menace and double meaning. The dialogue then becomes even more sinister when Hyde turns the tables and begins questioning Utterson by asking him how he knows him. It is only when we know the solution to the mystery that we realise how Hyde knows that Utterson is lying about Jekyll having given a description of Hyde.

Much of the tension in the dialogue is created by the way Utterson, the "detective" figure in the story, seeks to find out information by talking to the main characters involved. In Chapter 3, 'Dr Jekyll was quite at ease', Utterson is convinced that Jekyll is being blackmailed by Hyde. He says:

"Jekyll," said Utterson, "you know me: I am a man to be trusted. Make a clean breast of this in confidence and I make no doubt I can get you out of it."

The dialogue creates tension because Utterson does not "speak plainly" – he does not ask outright "Jekyll, are you being blackmailed?" – instead he urges his friend to "make a clean breast of this in confidence". In other words, he tells Jekyll that whatever it is that Jekyll is being blackmailed for can be confessed to him, and he will "get you out of it". The dialogue is emotional and secretive in atmosphere: this is a world where people do not share secrets easily and where the wrong words can ruin a man's reputation. Utterson is one of the few people in this world who can be trusted to keep a secret. And yet, Jekyll does not tell his friend what his secret is other than to reassure him that he is not being blackmailed.

Stevenson is wonderful at evoking a Gothic atmosphere in his descriptions of London; this is what is known as "urban Gothic" (see my chapter on this). If we examine the description of Soho in *The Carew Murder Case* we can see this:

> The dismal quarter of Soho seen under these changing glimpses, with its muddy ways, and slatternly passengers, and its lamps, which had never been extinguished or had been kindled afresh to combat this mournful reinvasion of darkness, seemed, in the lawyer's eyes, like a district of some city in a nightmare.

The use of adjectives like "dismal", "muddy", "slatternly" evoke a miserable, depressing and sinister atmosphere, while the visual image of the flickering, feeble lamps in this dark morning suggest a world where evil predominates. Meanwhile, the simile "like a district of some city in a nightmare" emphasizes a key idea in the novel: nightmares can become real; our worst dreams can become true.

Stevenson excels in various "set pieces": key scenes of action which are central to the plot of the story. These set-pieces are, in my view, the description of Poole's breaking into the laboratory in 'The Last Night' and Lanyon's description of Hyde's transformation into Jekyll. This latter description has set the template for many "transformation" scenes in literature and the movies:

> He put the glass to his lips and drank at one gulp. A cry followed; he reeled, staggered, clutched at the table and held on, staring with injected eyes, gasping with open mouth; and as I looked there came, I thought, a change—he seemed to swell—his face became suddenly black and the features seemed to melt and alter—and the next moment, I had sprung to my feet and leaped back against the wall, my arms raised to shield me from that prodigy, my mind submerged in terror.
>
> "O God!" I screamed, and "O God!" again and again; for there before my eyes—pale and shaken, and half fainting, and groping before him with his hands, like a man restored from death—there stood Henry Jekyll!

Here Stevenson uses powerful dynamic verbs "reeled, staggered, clutched...gasping" to describe the physical contortions and agony that Hyde undergoes as he changes back into Jekyll. Meanwhile, other dynamic verbs vividly convey the actual transformation: "swell...melt...alter". The effect of these verbs is to make the reader see a bewildering and disturbing transformation, while the use of descriptive noun phrases "injected eyes" and "opened mouth" brilliantly give a powerful visual image of someone appearing like they are being tortured. The use of colour "black" adds a very ambivalent edge to the description: does Jekyll literally go "black" as in "black skinned" or does he look like he's black because he's bruised? To then follow this description with the adjectives "pale and shaken" creates a strong contrast: Hyde had been having spasms but now is half-dead. Syntactically, Stevenson leaves the fatal name, Henry Jekyll, to the last words in the sentence to underline the shock Lanyon feels at seeing his former friend before him. Lanyon's responses only serve to suggest his shock and horror. He "sprung" to his feet, and "leapt back against the wall," raising his arms to hide the vision. The verbs here suggest violent, shocked movements. Thus the reader has two pictures in his head: he sees the transformation of Henry Jekyll but he also sees the terrified response of Lanyon. The short exclamation "Oh God!" also tells us of Lanyon's panic-stricken fear.

While this novel makes masterful use of language, it is interestingly in part about how some things – particularly horrifying things – cannot be described in language. There are a number of instances in the novel of people trying to describe Hyde but failing because words cannot capture the feelings people have when they see him. In 'Story of the Door', Enfield says:

> "No, sir; I can make no hand of it; I can't describe him. And it's not want of memory; for I declare I can see him this moment."

Stevenson's novel reaches beyond the words that are used to evoke the situation. He seems to be saying that language is not adequate to describe the feelings of horror that some people and situations create. This only adds to the chilling, dream-like atmosphere of the book.

TASKS

This is a good series of exercises to help you analyse the language of the book. Look at these different word classes (nouns, verbs, adjectives etc.) used in the story, and think about the connotations of the words: what do the words make you think, feel and see within the context of the novel? Look up the meanings of words you don't know.

NOUNS

Names: "Dr Henry Jekyll, Mr Edward Hyde, Mr. John Gabriel Utterson, Dr Hastie Lanyon." What do the sounds and connotations of these names suggest about the characters?

> POSSILBE ANSWER: The phrase "Dr" embodies "male respectability", power and prestige. Jekyll and Lanyon are both doctors and appear to be very respectable as a result. The irony is that Jekyll is the absolute opposite of "respectability" when he becomes "Mr Edward Hyde". For me, the word "Jekyll" has sinister overtones in that it sounds like "jackal" – a deadly wolfish animal. The word "Lanyon" has connotations of laziness and smugness for me, much like the character. Meanwhile the surname of "Hyde" is very important because it is, of course, a different spelling of "hide"; this is the surname Jekyll has given himself in his "alter ego" state. The lawyer in the novel, Utterson has the first name of "Gabriel" which suggests the Angel Gabriel, who was very good and I think it's no coincidence that Utterson is fundamentally a good man. His surname contains the word "utter" which means to "speak" or say something; Utterson often dares to say the unsayable and will listen to the unsayable when asks Jekyll to confess to him if he has something that he is being blackmailed for.

CONCRETE NOUNS

Describing the city: "thoroughfares, streets, lamps, fog, mist, labyrinths, and darkness." Why are these nouns used to describe the city?

> POSSIBLE ANSWER: Stevenson peppers his text with these concretes nouns to evoke both a "real" city of streets and thoroughfares but also suggest its nightmarish qualities: its "labyrinths" and "darkness". Both these concrete nouns are symbolic as well: the "labyrinth" is symbolic of the confusion that the reader and many of the characters feel because they are trapped in the maze of Jekyll's deceit. Similarly, the "darkness" of the city is symbolic of Jekyll's evil and deceit as well; he is swamped by the darkness of Hyde in much the same way the city is swamped by the foggy darkness of corruption and social injustice.

The house: "hallway, laboratory, cabinet, cheval-glass, phial." Why are these nouns emphasized in the descriptions of the house and laboratory?

> POSSIBLE ANSWER: Stevenson takes time to evoke Jekyll's house and laboratory by using concrete nouns that evoke both a respectable house and a working laboratory. Concrete nouns like "hallway" and "cabinet" suggest the luxury and spaciousness of Jekyll's house: this is such a big house that Hyde can go un-noticed while he lives for days at a time in the laboratory. Meanwhile, an old-fashioned noun phrase like "cheval-glass" suggests the vanity of Jekyll: this is a big mirror which is used to adjust clothing all over the body.

Nouns connected with the drugs/potions: "ebullition, salt, drugs, mixture."

> POSSIBLE ANSWER: The noun "ebullition" means "fizzing liquid": it is slightly archaic but it connotes the mysterious nature of Jekyll's potion; however it has scientific connotations and makes the drinking of the drug sound much less like something that might happen in a fairy-tale. If Stevenson had used "potion" consistently instead of this word, there would have been suggestions of Jekyll being rather like the wicked stepmother in *Snow White* who transforms herself from a beautiful woman into an old pedlar. The word "salt" and "drugs" both conjure a more scientific atmosphere as well.

RELIGIOUS LEXIS

"Devil, fiend, Satan, Juggernaut": Why are these religious nouns associated with Hyde?

> POSSIBLE ANSWER: Many critics have commented upon (Gray, 2004) the religious nature of the tale and how much Stevenson was influenced by the strict Christianity of his country, Scotland. Hyde is consistently linked with the "Devil": he is called by this emotive noun a number of times. He is the antithesis (opposite) of Jesus Christ. These religious nouns create a fevered, "Satanic" atmosphere and greatly increase the horror.

ABSTRACT NOUNS

"Duality, evil, horror, terror, good, goodness, dreams, nightmares, geniality." What role do these abstract nouns play in the novel?

> POSSIBLE ANSWER: These abstract nouns create the intellectual qualities of the book. The abstract noun "duality" is absolutely vital because it evokes the central theme of the novel, what Mighall (Mighall, 2003) calls the "double-consciousness" of Jekyll: he is a man of "two minds" and approaches to life, one which is wholly good and nice (Jekyll) and one which is wholly evil and anti-social (Hyde).

VERBS

What are the connotations of the following verbs and why are they important in the novel? Verbs connected with Mr Hyde: "sneering, stumping, trampling, murdering, striking, running, swearing, twitching."

> POSSIBLE ANSWER: The dynamic verbs associated with Hyde are very important in suggesting the violence of the character. He is even violent in the way he walks, being described as "stumping". He "tramples" on the girl at the beginning of the story and "strikes" Sir Danvers Carew to death: these dynamic verbs convey the power and evil of the man. Verbs like "whispering" describe the way he speaks: again this suggests his menace. He is not someone who needs to shout to be heard; people are transfixed by him and will listen even when he whispers.

Verbs connected with Jekyll: "sighing, crying, and pleading."

> POSSIBLE ANSWER: In stark contrast to Hyde, Jekyll often has rather "pathetic" verbs attached to him, particularly at the end of the book. He "sighs", "cries" and "pleads"; these verbs evoke how lost he is, how confused his situation is, and how desperate this once powerful and respectable man has become.

Verbs connected with Utterson: "seeking, dreaming, asking, and inquiring."

> POSSIBLE ANSWER: Utterson is always "seeking" the answer to the solution of the mystery of Hyde, but never

quite discovers it. The verbs connected with him suggest his curiosity and his inquiring nature: he is both fascinated and concerned by what has happened to his friend.

ADJECTIVES

What are the connotations of the following adjectives and why are they important in the novel? Adjectives connected with the city: "misty, foggy, dark, and black."

> POSSIBLE ANSWER: As has been said when talking about the concrete nouns connected with the city, much lexis suggests the mysterious and evil-nature of the city. These adjectives are both descriptive and symbolic: the "foggy" atmosphere not only tells us what the city looks like but also evokes the confusion people feel in this malign, nightmarish place.

Adjectives connected with Hyde: "displeasing, down-right detestable, deformed, sordid, evil, mis-shapen, small, energetic, ape-like, and troglodytic."

> POSSIBLE ANSWER: This is possibly the most interesting lexis to examine in the novel; each adjective connected with Hyde could be analysed at great length. The most important ones are connected with Hyde's physical appearance: he is "deformed" and "mis-shapen" and yet the irony is that there is never anything specific which categorically proves he is like this. In other words, while the adjectives are technically inaccurate in their physical description of him, these words evoke the "feeling" or "atmosphere" Hyde creates in the people that meet him. Hyde is someone who cannot be described: he has to be "felt" to be understood. This is a real paradox: he is a made-up character who "lives beyond the page"; he is the demon that lives within all of us. He is our worst aspects; the deformity of our souls. He is also the "primitive" side of our natures; he is described as "ape-like" and "troglodytic". In other words, he seems to convey what we were once like when we first evolved as humans: he is our violent, unfettered ancestor who would club anyone he didn't like to death without any feelings of guilt.

ADVERBS

What are the connotations of the following adverbs and why are they important in the novel? Adverbs connected with people talking: "hoarsely, peevishly, and complainingly."

POSSIBLE ANSWER: These adverbs suggest the nightmarish qualities of Hyde: he is "hoarse". There is something "painful" to hear in his voice. Many people in the novel are irritated or anxious; they behave "peevishly" and "complainingly".

DIFFERENT LITERARY STYLES

Look at the way Stevenson uses different literary forms in the novel. At times, the book uses "third-person" narration – people are described in the "third person", i.e. "he/she/it/they". When does this happen and what is the effect of this?

At other times, Stevenson makes use of first person narration, using letters, first-hand testimonies, wills and confessions to show what is happening. When does this happen and why do you think he switches "person" like this?

POSSIBLE ANSWER: Stevenson brings real variety to the novel by using so many different styles: the reader is never bored by being subjected to one style for long. He also provides the novel with what we might call "veracity" or the "ring of truth" by using forms which are largely "non-fictional", that is they are used to convey truths and facts. For example, Jekyll's notes to the chemist convey very vividly his desperation for drugs, while the first hand testimonies of Lanyon and Enfield turn what are actually rather unbelievable events into ones that are believable because they are written in a non-fictional form.

6 Characterisations

It is important to realise that the characters in the novel are not "real people" but invented creations. The author has invented them to engage our interest in their stories, to make us feel certain emotions towards them, to use them as a way to explore certain issues. A good literary critic must think about the techniques an author uses to make a character interesting, and the thoughts, feelings and images a character provokes in the reader's mind.

Dr Jekyll

Dr Jekyll is a complex character. He is a rich man who lives what appears to be a very "respectable" life as a scientist, except that this appearance of respectability hides a darker side. In his confession, he talks about having a "dual" nature from an early age: he indulges in things that are not respectable in the society he lives in. We never really learn what these things are but we can guess: he probably likes having sex with people who were not deemed as suitable partners during that time.

Stevenson's first description of him is informative:

> Dr. Jekyll was no exception; and as he now sat on the opposite side of the fire—a large, well-made, smooth-faced man of fifty, with something of a stylish cast perhaps, but every mark of capacity and kindness—you could see by his looks that he cherished for Mr. Utterson a sincere and warm affection.

It's important to note that Jekyll is a kind man who does "good works": he helps out the poor, various charities and religious causes. He is the embodiment of Victorian respectability and seems to take pleasure in helping people and being a good friend. Except, of course, this is, to a degree, a "sham", a "façade": he appears this way, but in reality he is not. Stevenson uses him as a way of exploring the hypocrisy of Victorian England: this is a world where appearances mean everything and, as a result, many rich people are being blackmailed because they are not as "squeaky clean" as they pretend to be. Jekyll believes that becoming Hyde is wonderful because it allows him to be the person he could never be if he was Jekyll: he can be violent, anti-social, and can go to places of "sin" and "vice" that might mean Jekyll's disgrace if he were seen in them. In his confession, this passage is perhaps the most revealing of Jekyll:

> Not that I dreamed of resuscitating Hyde; the bare idea of that would startle **me** to frenzy: no, it was in my own person that I was once more tempted to trifle with my conscience; and it was as an ordinary secret sinner that I at last fell before the assaults of temptation.

After deciding to stop being Hyde, Jekyll finds he can't stop himself in indulging in Hyde's pleasures as himself and, as a consequence, becomes an "ordinary secret sinner" who "fell before the assaults of temptation". The language here is important: Jekyll sees "temptation" or desire as an "assault"; it is like being attacked. This shows how terrified Jekyll is of his secret desires. What are they though? We never really learn in the novel, but in various filmed versions of the book we see him acting like a paedophile, a sex maniac and a psycho-path. Part of the book's power may be that we never learn what he has been doing, thus leaving us to imagine his depravity.

Jekyll is "vindictive" and settles old scores in the novel. This is particularly the case with Lanyon. Just before Hyde turns back into Jekyll in front of Lanyon, Jekyll speaking as Hyde says:

> And now, you who have so long been bound to the most narrow and material views, you who have denied the virtue of transcendental medicine, you who have derided your superiors —behold!

Here we see Jekyll "tell off" Lanyon for holding "narrow and material views", in other words for being blinkered and unimaginative. He calls himself a "superior" to Lanyon and makes it very clear that Lanyon was wrong to "deride" or mock him. This is a clear example of Jekyll settling an old score: although he pretended to be relaxed about Lanyon criticising his scientific methods earlier on in the novel, we learn here, through the voice of Hyde, that he definitely is not.

It important to note that Hyde is Jekyll; this seems like an obvious point but it is easy to forget. Jekyll is portrayed in a psychologically convincing fashion: he is a fully-fleshed out character who reveals a striking array of different emotions and personas. The portrayal is psychological because we see that when Jekyll represses his inner-most desires he causes serious problems for himself: Hyde has been created out of his repressed desires. This is most clearly seen with the murder of Carew in Jekyll's confession: he tells us that before the murder he had been deliberately trying to avoid taking the potion and that when he did, the potion had a doubly strong effect; his repressed anger came out in a terrifying fashion.

Questions

Why and how is Jekyll a complex character?

Why is Stevenson's characterisation of Jekyll a "psychological" portrayal?

POSSIBLE ANSWERS in brief & bold

Why and how is Jekyll a complex character? **Jekyll is complex because we learn by the end of the story that there are many sides to him. There is the "good", the side that helps charities and the poor and is a loyal friend; there is the "respectable", the part of him that wants to be seen as "decent" and "upstanding"; and then there is the side that enjoys inflicting pain upon people, the sadistic side; and there is also the "undignified" side, the side that does things that no respectable person would condone.**

Why is Stevenson's characterisation of Jekyll a "psychological" portrayal? **The portrait is psychological because Stevenson really tries to work out WHY Jekyll behaves in this way: we see in Jekyll's 'Full Statement' an explanation of Jekyll's decline; we learn how Jekyll felt he had Hyde under control to begin with, but then Hyde becomes "monstrous" as Jekyll takes more and more of the drug. This is a very psychological portrait of Jekyll because we see how he doesn't suddenly turn into an evil monster: it happened by degrees.**

Mr Hyde

Utterson's first meeting with Hyde is revealing. Stevenson writes:

> Mr. Hyde was pale and dwarfish, he gave an impression of deformity without any nameable malformation, he had a

displeasing smile, he had borne himself to the lawyer with a sort of murderous mixture of timidity and boldness, and he spoke with a husky, whispering and somewhat broken voice; all these were points against him, but not all of these together could explain the hitherto unknown disgust, loathing and fear with which Mr. Utterson regarded him.

Hyde is, in many ways, the opposite of Jekyll. Where Jekyll is tall and kind-looking, Hyde is "dwarfish" and has a "displeasing smile" that has a "murderous mixture of timidity and boldness". He clearly smiles in a perverted or unpleasant fashion, and is both cowardly and bold. Many film versions of the book do not capture this aspect of Hyde, making him appear quite a brave but psychopathic character: he isn't brave at all. When he is confronted with what he has done to the little girl, he backs down and pays the family compensation because he is frightened of what they might do to him. When he suddenly appears in Regent's Park at the end of the novel, he is terrified of being caught and hung.

On the other hand, he is not afraid of getting away with what he can; he is not worried about what people think of him. He does not observe the normal rules of politeness: he hits people he doesn't like, and appears to dislike people for irrational reasons – we see this particularly with Sir Danvers Carew. He is probably highly sexual. We are told that he is "troglodytic"; this means that he is like a cave man. In Stevenson's time, this was probably code for being highly sexual (Mighall, 2003 & Luckhurst, 2006): it was thought by the Victorians that our ancestors behaved like apes and had no sexual inhibitions.

His true character comes out towards the end of the novel when we learn of his emotions towards Jekyll:

> The hatred of Hyde for Jekyll was of a different order. His terror of the gallows drove him continually to commit temporary suicide, and return to his subordinate station of a part instead of a person; but he loathed **the** necessity, he loathed the despondency into which Jekyll was now fallen, and he resented the dislike with which he was himself regarded. Hence the ape-like tricks that he would play me, scrawling in my own hand blasphemies on the pages of my books, burning the letters and destroying the portrait of my father; and indeed, had it not been for his fear of death, he would long ago have ruined himself in order to involve me in the ruin. But his love of me is wonderful; I go further: I, who sicken and freeze at the mere thought of him, when I recall the abjection and passion of this attachment,

and when I know how he fears my power to cut him off by suicide, I find it in my heart to pity him.

We learn here that Hyde temporarily "commits suicide" – in other words he drinks the potion that makes him Jekyll – only because he wants to avoid being hung, not because he wants to be Jekyll again. He hates Jekyll's "despondency" or depression suggesting that Hyde is a high-spirited, bizarrely joyful person: he is described as being in a "transport of glee" as he murders Carew. Although it has to be said there is a problem here because Jekyll uses the pronoun "I" to describe Hyde's feelings while he is killing Carew, thereby implying that Jekyll felt this way too. He is also a joker who loves to swear and desecrate things: he writes "blasphemies" in the pages of Jekyll's books, he burns the portrait of Jekyll's father. There is almost something pathetic about Hyde for all his horrible selfishness: he is like an unruly child.

It is important to note that Hyde, according to Jekyll's 'Full Statement' is not immediately evil. We learn when first appeared what Hyde does is "undignified" but his pleasures become "monstrous" as he gains in power. In other words, Hyde seems to gain strength by being allowed to exist, and progressively becomes more and more violent. When Jekyll gives up taking the drug for two months after being shocked to find that he has woken up as Hyde, Hyde comes back even stronger and more uncontrolled after Jekyll takes the potion again, and murders Carew as a result. In fact he becomes so strong that he appears without Jekyll taking the potion: once Jekyll has decided to stop being Hyde altogether, Hyde springs back to life in Regent's Park without Jekyll ingesting the drug. From then onwards, Jekyll has to swallow stronger and stronger doses of the drug to stop being Hyde. This suggests that Hyde rather than being a fully-rounded character is an "aspect" or element of Jekyll: a Freudian critic might argue that he is the "Id" or the inner-desires of Jekyll which becomes stronger the longer he is allowed to exist. A religious interpretation might be that Hyde is the "Devil", the inner "evil" of mankind, who thrives when God is ignored or deliberately disobeyed. Some other critics, called "cultural theorists", have examined the culture that allows someone like Hyde to thrive and have argued that Hyde is a product of the society that he lives in (see Katherine Linehan in Literary Criticism chapter); he is allowed to get away with his crimes because someone with money and anonymity can. It is only when he angers the upper-classes with the murder of Carew that he is actually stopped.

Questions

What does Hyde look like? Why do people say that he seems "deformed"? Why is he compared to being an "ape" or a cave man at times? What does Hyde symbolise?

POSSIBLE ANSWERS in brief & bold

What does Hyde look like and how does he act? **Hyde is small and muscular, and appears in some way "deformed". He is described as "stumping", that is, moving by violently putting his feet on the ground. When he speaks he seems to "whisper" in a "hoarse" fashion.**

Why do people say that he seems "deformed"? **Although he does not explicitly look ugly, everyone who meets him feels there is something abnormal about him. Just his presence makes people feel "icy". It could be that he arouses a primitive feeling of fear in people, in the same way wild animals or snakes make people feel afraid.**

Why is he compared to being an "ape" or a cave man at times? **Stevenson, like many writers of the time, was very affected by the science of evolution developed by Charles Darwin. Hyde seems at times to be a "throwback" to when humans were "ape-like": it almost as if Jekyll has accessed our evolutionary past when he takes the potion** (Mighall, 2003).

What does Hyde symbolise? **Hyde symbolises different things to different critics. For people interpreting the book as a Christian "allegory" (a long symbolic religious story) he represents the Devil, and all the temptations of the Devil and evil. There is a great deal of religious imagery in the book which suggests this interpretation has validity: Hyde is compared to the devil and he himself, when he is taking the potion before Lanyon, referencing the name of Satan.**

Mr Utterson

One could argue that Utterson is the "protagonist" – the main character -- of the novel in that he plays the detective figure searching out for the clues as to what is happening to Jekyll. In the first chapter Stevenson describes him in this way:

But he had an approved tolerance for others; sometimes wondering, almost with envy, at the high pressure of spirits involved in their misdeeds; and in any extremity inclined to help rather than to reprove. "I incline to Cain's heresy," he used to say quaintly: "I let my brother go to the devil in his own way." In this character, it was frequently his fortune to be the last reputable acquaintance and the last good influence in the lives of downgoing men. And to such as these, so long as they came about his chamber, he never marked a shade of change in his demeanour.

Utterson is a boring man who does not seem to have the desires, dreams or contradictions of Jekyll. He does not judge people however -- but helps them. He lets people do what they want without interfering. This is what makes him an excellent character to investigate the case of Jekyll because he is not easily shocked: he helps "downgoing" men, that is, people who are losing their reputations for respectability. In the novel, we see him being very persistent: he tracks down Hyde after much waiting around for him at his door. We see him being caring: he tries continually to help Jekyll. He is also non-judgemental, offering to listen to Jekyll if he has anything to confess. He is also decisive: he makes the decision to knock down the door to Jekyll's room in order to see where Jekyll is. Ultimately, it is his desire to find out the truth about Jekyll which leads to Jekyll's destruction.

In literary terms, Utterson serves as a good counter-point to the extremes of Jekyll and Hyde and provides the narrative with a good "anchor" in that his realistic, ordinary approach to life contrasts greatly with Jekyll and Hyde's fantastical experiments and misdemeanours.

Questions
Why could you argue that Utterson is the main protagonist in the novel? How and why does he behave like a detective?

Answers in brief and bold
Why could you argue that Utterson is the main protagonist in the novel? **For the first half of the novel, before Jekyll gives his 'Full Statement', Utterson is the main character in that the reader follows his journey as he gradually uncovers the truth about Jekyll. Some critics have argued that he ultimately destroys Jekyll in his quest for the truth because Jekyll/Hyde takes the poison that kills himself after Utterson says he will knock down the door.**

How and why does he behave like a detective? **Utterson operates like a detective because he is continually looking for clues as to what is going on with Hyde: he takes some time to search for Hyde, he thinks about the problem of Jekyll's will, he questions Poole, Lanyon and Jekyll himself about what is happening with Jekyll, he finds clues such as the broken walking stick, and he confronts Jekyll/Hyde by breaking down the door to his laboratory. All of these things make him like your "classic detective", except of course there were very few detective novels before this one was written. Some people have argued that Stevenson invented the form of the detective novel with this book.**

Dr Lanyon

This is an early description of Lanyon:

> Dr. Lanyon sat alone over his wine. This was a hearty, healthy, dapper, red-faced gentleman, with a shock of hair prematurely white, and a boisterous and decided manner.

In many ways, Lanyon is very similar to Jekyll in that he is a respectable, wealthy scientist who has a happy life. However, he has disassociated himself with Jekyll because of Jekyll's scientific experiments which Lanyon believes are "unscientific balderdash". Lanyon is a "smug" and patronising man who believes he knows best. He learns a terrible lesson when he sees Jekyll turn into Hyde. After this time, all his certainties about life are shattered and he becomes a broken man:

> He had his death-warrant written legibly upon his face. The rosy man had grown pale; his flesh had fallen away; he was visibly balder and older; and yet it was not so much these tokens of a swift physical decay that arrested the lawyer's notice, as a look in the eye and quality of manner that seemed to testify to some deep-seated terror of the mind.

Lanyon seems to represent the self-satisfied certainties of Victorian England: he appears to be someone who thinks he knows it all and then learns to his cost that he does not. There is a suggestion too that he too may have tried the potion or may be tempted to use it: the "terror of the mind" is his horror that he is just like Jekyll and harbours secret, terrifying desires.

Lanyon serves an important role in the novel in that he witnesses Hyde's transformation into Jekyll; Stevenson deliberately engineers the narrative so that it is a scientist who witnesses this transformation because a scientist is a more trustworthy observer than someone who already believes in "supernatural" transformations.

Questions

How does Stevenson present Dr Lanyon?
Why is it Lanyon who observes Hyde's transformation into Hyde?

POSSIBLE ANSWERS in brief & bold

How does Stevenson present Dr Lanyon? **Stevenson presents Lanyon as a self-satisfied scientist who is a "materialist", i.e. he doesn't believe in mystical transformations or magic. He has a very happy and successful life in Cavendish Square, one of the wealthiest areas of London. His confidence in his scientific views is shattered when he witnesses Hyde's transformation into Jekyll. Stevenson uses a mixture of description, dialogue and first-hand testimony to make Lanyon a plausible and interesting character. Initially, we hear about Lanyon's beliefs that Jekyll's scientific methods are "balderdash", thus setting him up in what seems to be a minor conflict of opinion with Jekyll. However, we learn later that Jekyll has been greatly angered by Lanyon's dismissal of his science and that he achieves a kind of revenge upon him when he shows how Hyde can change into Jekyll. Lanyon's shock and horror at having his logical, scientific beliefs shattered ultimately kill him.**
Why is it Lanyon who observes Hyde's transformation into Hyde?
Stevenson gives the narrative more "credibility" or makes it more believable by having Lanyon observe Hyde's transformation because Lanyon is a skeptical, rational scientist who is a "truthful" observer. If a mystical person had seen the change, then we might have doubted his word because he would merely be endorsing what he already believes. However, Lanyon has to deny all his previous beliefs in order to say that the transformation really happened.

Poole

Poole is Jekyll's elderly butler who shows surprising strength in knocking down Jekyll's stout door. He is the embodiment of the Victorian servant: he is loyal and obedient even when his master's demands are outrageous. Like Lanyon he has all his certainties about life shattered: he comes to believe that his master's supposed friend, Hyde, has murdered him. He cannot act though without the support of his social superiors. This is why he asks Utterson to visit in the chapter 'The Last Night': although he would like to break down the door to Jekyll's room he knows he doesn't have the authority, but Utterson his social superior does.

Poole serves an important literary function in the novel in that he is used to heighten the sense of mystery and suspense. We see this in 'Search for Mr Hyde' when he tells Utterson that the servants have to obey Hyde and that Hyde is a familiar figure in the household. Most strikingly, he generates a huge amount of suspense in 'The Last Night' by the way he suddenly appears and says that there has been "foul play" to Utterson: the fact that he, of all people, is so upset shows how terrible the situation is. Thus we can see how Stevenson uses his character to convey a sense of horror at Jekyll's predicament: if Poole can be upset then we all should be. The way Poole calls Hyde "it" is particularly chilling: Poole dehumanises Hyde in a way that no one else has been willing to do. He seems to realise that Hyde is not the same as the human race. Other people like Lanyon, Utterson and Enfield are more easily fooled by the social codes of the day and view Hyde as a gentleman, if a bad one. Poole though knows that Hyde is different. His theory that his master has been "made away with" turns out to be the closest guess of all. In such a way, we could argue that despite the fact that Poole speaks in "slang", he is actually one of the more intelligent characters.

His character also illustrates how Hyde has managed not only to destroy and abuse people, but his actions have threatened the social order of the society. Utterson notes with horror that it is not good that all the servants are not doing their jobs anymore; furthermore, we see Poole, who should be preserving his master's household, destroying his master's door with an axe.

Questions
What function does Poole serve in the narrative?

What evidence is there that Poole is actually quite perceptive and intelligent?

POSSIBLE ANSWERS in brief & bold

What function does Poole serve in the narrative? **Poole is important in the narrative because he helps heighten the suspense considerably. At first, the introduction of Poole helps heighten the mystery about the connection between Hyde and Jekyll because he tells Utterson that Jekyll has given orders for the servants to obey Hyde. In 'The Last Night' Poole creates a great deal of the suspense by appearing so worried about Jekyll, and theorising that he has been "made away with". By calling Hyde "it", he creates a sense of horror regarding Hyde, suggesting Hyde's inhuman qualities.**

What evidence is there that Poole is actually quite perceptive and intelligent? **Of all the characters in the novel, it is Poole who gets closest to the truth when he suggests that Jekyll has been "made away with" or murdered by Hyde. This is something that Utterson doesn't believe; preferring to think Jekyll is ill and needs drugs. Poole also subtly engineers the breaking down of Jekyll's door by revealing the truth about the situation to Utterson in stages, and not all at once. This suggests he knows Utterson well and realises that he can't tell Utterson the full extent of knowledge until Utterson has witnessed Jekyll's house himself.**

7 Themes

Good versus evil

This might seem to be an obvious theme because one could argue that Jekyll represents "good" and Hyde represents "evil". However, a close reading of the novel shows that this theme is more complicated than that. In his full statement of the case, Jekyll confesses:

> I was no more myself when I laid **(put)** aside restraint **(self-control)** and plunged **(dived into)** in shame, than

when I laboured **(worked)**, in the eye of day, at the furtherance **(development)** of knowledge or the relief of sorrow and suffering.

When Jekyll "plunges" into "shame" we must assume that he is behaving in an "evil" fashion, while when he works for the "relief of suffering", he is doing "good". In other words, Jekyll is both "evil" and "good"; the two elements sit side by side within him. It is not a question of "good versus evil" but more the case that good needs evil to exist and vice versa. This is a radical thought and one that questions certain religious ideas which state that God is wholly good. By this account, this could not be the case because goodness only exists because its opposite exists. Thus we can say that there appears to be a fight within Jekyll between his good and evil side, but, as we have seen, it is more complicated than saying they are opposing forces. The novel is full of Christian imagery which references things which many Christian people regard as "sinful" or evil. There are many things to note that Jekyll does that are, in his eyes, sinful; he calls them "undignified pleasures", "irregularities", and a "gaiety of disposition" for which he feels a sense of "shame". Some critics believe that Stevenson's religious upbringing is important here in that he was taught to feel a sense of "shame" at the pleasures of the body: eating, drinking, sensuality, and sex. The strict Scottish Calvinism which Stevenson's family adhered to believed that the body or the flesh was essentially evil and needed to be constantly punished in order to be "good".

Question
In what way does the novel explore the theme of good and evil?
Please re-read the above section to find the answer.

The duality of man

This is Stevenson's main theme: the "two-sided" aspect of man. He shows that co-existing within all human beings are both the good and the bad:

> It was on the moral side, and in my own person, that I learned to recognise the thorough and primitive duality of man; I saw that, of the two natures that contended in the field of my consciousness, even if I could rightly be said to be either, it was only because I was radically both; and from an early date, even before the course of my scientific discoveries had begun to suggest the most naked possibility of such a miracle, I had learned to dwell with pleasure, as a beloved daydream, on the thought of the separation of these elements.

Henry Jekyll's great idea is that he can "separate" the two sides of man: the animal and the divine, the good and the bad, the ugly and the beautiful. However, his idea is revealed to be naïve because the author shows that the two elements are inter-dependent – as has already been discussed in the section "Good versus evil". This duality is "primitive" because all that is good about man is spoilt by the bad side. Therefore Jekyll proposes separating the bad side off entirely. This was a problem that preoccupied many Victorians who agreed with Darwin's theory of evolution but were horrified that there might be something "ape-like" about their beings, their personalities, their bodies. So Jekyll's quest is very much the secret quest of many people of the time: a quest to "get rid of" the "animal" and "primitive" side, to expunge the "ape" in the "man". His narrative reveals that this can't be done because the "ape" or "Hyde side" takes over.

Question
In what way does the novel explore the theme of the duality of man?
Please re-read the above section to find the answer.

Appearance versus reality

A key theme in this book is the lengths men will go to appear respectable: to hide their inner-most desires. We learn from Utterson that he is well aware that many men are black-mailed for the "indiscretions of their youth". This is a society where "appearance is all" (Luckhurst, 2006): if it was learnt that you were actually homosexual or had no money then you would be ruined.

Some critics think that Utterson suspects that Jekyll is being blackmailed by Hyde because he is homosexual. Homosexuality was a crime in England until 1968 and men were jailed for it, most famously an acquaintance of Stevenson's, the writer Oscar Wilde, was jailed a few years after the publication of this book for homosexuality. His entire career was ruined. This book is radical in that it suggests that within all men lurk secret desires: in other words, many so-called respectable people lead "phoney" lives, pretending to be people they are not.

Question
In what ways does the novel explore the theme of appearance versus reality?
Please re-read the above section to find the answer.

The limits of science

This theme is clearly exemplified in the characterisation of Lanyon who is a self-satisfied scientist who has all his beliefs shattered when he sees Hyde transform into Jekyll. Stevenson seems to be suggesting that modern, rational science simply isn't adequate to explain the world. Let's look at this quote in order to explore this issue:

> "We had," was the reply. "But it is more than ten years since Henry Jekyll became too fanciful for me. He began to go wrong, wrong in mind; and though of course I continue to take an interest in him for old sake's sake, as they say, I see and I have seen devilish little of the man. Such unscientific balderdash," added the doctor, flushing suddenly purple, "would have estranged Damon and Pythias."

Here we see Dr Lanyon become annoyed at the thought of Dr Jekyll's science: he feels that Jekyll has been conducting experiments which are "unscientific balderdash", in other words are worthless rubbish. He says that their disagreement would have made even the best of friends, Damon and Pythias, fall out. We, the reader, however find it difficult to see why this would be the case: certainly Utterson doesn't regard their disagreement as important and sees it as an irrelevance. However, in the context of the novel, it turns out that their disagreement is vital because we learn that Jekyll has actually shown that Lanyon's "narrow" and "material" views of the world are wrong, and that transformation into another creature is possible. Thus we can see that the novel is, in a way, showing that science is limited in its ability to explain the mysteries of life and the human character, which are far more complex than science would have us believe.

Question
In what way does the novel explore the theme of the limits of science?
Please re-read the above section to find the answer.

The "nightmarish" city

One could argue that the city is a personality in the novel in its own right. At certain critical points in the novel, Stevenson takes great care to describe the atmosphere and physical environment of London. Some critics have argued that he is actually describing his hometown of Edinburgh in Scotland rather than London because Stevenson's London has a split personality in much the same way that Edinburgh had -- and Jekyll does too. Edinburgh was divided into the "Old" and "New Town": the "Old Town" was extremely run-down and very much like where Hyde lives, while the "New Town" had houses similar to Jekyll's: grand, large, well-proportioned. Of course, Jekyll's house has Hyde's living quarters at the back so we can see how the two sides of the city – the respectable and the disgraceful – are inter-connected. It's worth examining his descriptions of the city in detail. Here's an account in 'The Carew Murder' of Utterson and the police visiting Hyde's flat:

As the cab drew up before the address indicated, the fog lifted a little and showed him a dingy street, a gin palace, a low French eating house, a shop for the retail of penny numbers and twopenny salads, many ragged children huddled in the doorways, and many women of many different nationalities passing out, key in hand, to have a morning glass; and the next moment the fog settled down again upon that part, as brown as umber, and cut him off from his blackguardly surroundings. This was the home of Henry Jekyll's favourite;

The description would have provoked the fears of middle-class Victorians because it evokes child poverty, prostitution and immigration. Stevenson describes children who are "ragged", in other words dressed in rags, and who appear to have no parents or proper guardians: they are possibly orphans who have been abandoned. He talks about a number of shops and restaurants all of which are unpleasant: there is a "gin palace" which is place to buy very cheap and strong alcohol, a "low French eating house" which is a nasty, inexpensive restaurant, and a shop where you can get very cheap takeaway food "twopenny salads" and stories of sensational crimes, "penny numbers". He talks about women who have their own "keys" to their houses; this would have been a signal that they were prostitutes or "corrupted" women to Victorian readers because normally only husbands were allowed to carry front door keys (Luckhurst, 2006). The surroundings are described as "blackguardly"; they are perceived as wicked, morally corrupt, and evil. This is the world that Hyde thrives in because he can "hide" within it.

Question
In what way does the novel explore the theme of the city being like a nightmare?
Please re-read the above section to find the answer.

Desire

A dominating theme of the novel is the nature of Henry Jekyll's desires. He has a number of desires which are contradictory: he wants to appear respectable but also to indulge in violent and possibly sexual behaviour; he wants to have good friends and yet he doesn't want to share his "secret" life with them. This passage from his "Testament" is instructive:

> And indeed the worst of my faults was a certain impatient gaiety of disposition, such as has made the happiness of many, but such as I found it hard to reconcile with my imperious desire to carry my head high, and wear a more than commonly grave countenance before the public.

More than any other passage this tells us what he is really like: he has a "gaiety" of disposition. In Stevenson's time, "gaiety" was slang for men who liked to sleep with many women, while disposition meant "character" (Luckhurst, 2006). But this desire to live the life of a "playboy" was not really permitted for someone who wanted to wear a "grave countenance" – or respectable face – in public. In other words, his desires are utterly contradictory. This is, at root, his major problem.

Question
In what way does the novel explore the theme of desire?
Please re-read the above section to find the answer.

Repression

Shortly after Stevenson wrote his novella, the psycho-analyst Sigmund Freud developed a theory for human nature which suggested that our characters are composed of three key elements: the "Id", which represents our true desires whatever they may be, the "Ego" which is the part of the mind that seeks to satisfy the "Id", and the "Superego" which the part of our mind which obeys the rules of society rather than our own desires. The critic William Gray (p. 54, Gray, 2004) points out that Henry Jekyll's predicament lends itself to a "Freudian" analysis in that it's clear that Jekyll's "Superego" which is, at bottom, the problem, because it crushes his true desires, and represses (or tries to ignore them) to such an extent that the "Id" forces itself upon when he takes a drug which takes away his inhibitions. Stevenson makes it clear that when Jekyll really represses his true desires, when they eventually surface they are much stronger than they would have been if he had allowed them to naturally express themselves. This is very obviously seen in Jekyll's description of the murder of Sir Danvers Carew:

> My devil had been long caged, he came out roaring. I was conscious, even when I took the draught, of a more unbridled, a more furious propensity to ill.

Jekyll had "caged" or imprisoned his "devil" – his innermost desires – and, as a result of this repression, it comes out "roaring" like a terrible monster. It is fascinating to note Jekyll's use of pronouns here. Sometimes, he describes Hyde in the third person as "he" but here he uses the first person "I" which makes it very clear that it is Jekyll who is essentially committing these crimes – not Hyde. This is obviously because Jekyll is Hyde: but this fact is easy to forget unless you read the text very carefully. Jekyll's desires are "unbridled" and he has a "furious propensity to ill": his desires have totally taken over him; there is no "Superego" to stop him doing what he really wants to do. However, it is clear that his violence has been generated by the repression that his Superego has imposed upon him: because he has repressed his desires, when they are expressed they all the more violent. Thus we can see Stevenson exploring a theory of repression here which anticipates the theories of Sigmund Freud.

Question
In what way does the novel explore the theme of repression?
Please re-read the above section to find the answer.

Dreams and nightmares

Linked to the theory of repression is Stevenson's exploration of dream-like states. The book itself was the outcome of a nightmare so it is possibly not surprising that the whole of the novel has the quality of a nightmare. Many of the most famous images in the book are dream-like in nature: the violence of Hyde trampling on the girl and murdering Carew; the discovery of the suicidal Hyde's small, twitching body in Jekyll's clothes; and the way Hyde magically transforms into Jekyll in such a violent and surprising fashion. One of the scariest images in the book is a description of Utterson's dream:

as he lay and tossed in the gross darkness of the night and the curtained room, Mr. Enfield's tale went by before his mind in a scroll of lighted pictures. He would be aware of the great field of lamps of a nocturnal city; then of the figure of a man walking swiftly; then of a child running from the doctor's; and then these met, and that human Juggernaut trod the child down and passed on regardless of her screams. Or else he would see a room in a rich house, where his friend lay asleep, dreaming and smiling at his dreams; and then the door of that room would be opened, the curtains of the bed plucked apart, the sleeper recalled, and lo! there would stand by his side a figure to whom power was given, and even at that dead hour, he must rise and do its bidding. The figure in these two phases haunted the lawyer all night

The image of this "faceless figure" is possibly even more unpleasant than the actual appearance of Hyde: this is a truly nightmarish image of inhuman brutality. It's a dream-like image which haunts the reader: there is something particularly disturbing about faceless figures that chase after children for no apparent reason other than to commit violence. The idea of such a figure hovering over our beds is also extremely unpleasant: we're at our most vulnerable when we're asleep.

Question
In what way does the novel explore the theme of dreams and nightmares?
Please re-read the above section to find the answer.

Friendship

Friendship doesn't appear to be an immediately obvious theme in the book, but it is an important one. After all, it is Utterson's friendship for Dr Jekyll that compels him to investigate his case at some considerable danger to himself; this is particularly the case when he breaks down the door to Jekyll's cabinet in 'The Last Night'; there is no telling what Hyde might have done at this point . It is important to note that Utterson is the opposite of a "fair weather" friend: he tells Jekyll that he can confess his sins to him without fear that he will judge him or disown him. And yet, Jekyll consistently rejects the chance to have a "deeper" friendship with

Utterson because it is clear that he enjoys his secret life too much. Jekyll's true friendship is with Edward Hyde, the dark side of his character. Although this friendship is very troubled and ultimately destroys both of them, it is a very deep friendship; each man knows the truth about each other. Lanyon is presented by Stevenson as a man who is ruined by his friendship with Jekyll: after he carries out Jekyll's instructions to fetch the drugs for him in 'Dr Lanyon's Narrative', Lanyon decides to look at Hyde take the drug, despite Hyde's warning. What he sees ultimately results in his death, even though he disowns Jekyll as a friend. Jekyll has broken the bonds of friendship with Lanyon because he has revealed himself as he really is: degraded, corrupted, evil. Lanyon cannot endure having a friend of this type.

This prompts the thought as to what would have happened if it had been Utterson that Hyde had transformed into Jekyll before. One suspects that Utterson would not have been destroyed by the revelation in the way Lanyon is because Utterson is a less pretension, pompous man, who already has a pretty jaundiced view of human nature. Thus we can see Stevenson reveals to us the different variety of friends one encounters in life: the judgemental friends like Lanyon who reject people if they are not who they believe them to be; the more forgiving friends like Utterson; and finally, the friend we make with ourselves in our own minds such as Jekyll makes with Hyde. If we see ourselves as, at root, as a bad person we clearly form destructive relationships with ourselves, and set ourselves on the road to ruin.

Question
In what way does the novel explore the theme of friendship?
Please re-read the above section to find the answer.

Secrecy & blackmail

Enfield, a friend of Utterson's, points out where Hyde lives and says this to Utterson:

> "Black Mail House is what I call the place with the door, in consequence. Though even that, you know, is far from explaining all," he added, and with the words fell into a vein of musing

Clearly Enfield is well aware of the concept of blackmail. As a respectable man about town who probably enjoyed "capers" – as he calls them – in his youth, Enfield may well be worried that he may be blackmailed at some point. In Victorian Britain, it was very important to appear "respectable" and "morally upright" if you were going to succeed in society; if it was known that you had slept with the "wrong person", or were homosexual, or a bankrupt, then it was very likely that you would be sacked from your job, rejected by your friends, and generally cast out from wealthy society. As a result, people could make considerable amounts of money by blackmailing respectable, rich people and threatening to expose their secrets if they did not pay up. There were very few people that a "gentleman" with a secret could trust. One such person is Utterson. This becomes clear when Utterson speaks to Jekyll alone in the chapter 'Dr Jekyll was quite at ease':

> "Jekyll," said Utterson, "you know me: I am a man to be trusted. Make a clean breast of this in confidence; and I make no doubt I can get you out of it."

Utterson makes an offer to Jekyll by saying that he can speak to him "in confidence", i.e. in secret. Utterson is possibly worried that Jekyll is being blackmailed because he had a homosexual relationship with Hyde, or because Hyde, looking much younger than Jekyll, is Jekyll's illegitimate son (Mighall, 2003). Jekyll reassures Utterson that his case is not as bad this and that he can get rid of Hyde at any time he wants. The wonderful thing about Hyde from Jekyll's perspective is that, while he has to remain a secret, there is no threat that he will be blackmailed for doing what he wants to do. Hyde has been created because Jekyll lives in a world where it is very easy to be blackmailed: he can't go out openly and sleep with prostitutes or do things like gamble without worrying that someone might see him and he'll get blackmailed as a result. In a world where people can do what they want, there would be no need for Hyde.

Question
In what way does the novel explore the themes of secrecy and blackmail?
Please re-read the above section to find the answer.

8 Imagery, symbols and motifs

One of the most striking aspects of the novel is its use of repeated images. For the purposes of definition we could say that imagery refers to all the poetic devices a writer uses, while a symbol is an image which represents a particular concept or idea, and a "motif" is a repeated image or symbol which is threaded throughout the novel.

The door

The first chapter of the book is called 'Story of the Door' and describes Hyde's scruffy, derelict door in detail. The door here symbolizes the gateway to more evil world; it is the access point for violence and unpleasantness. Its very aspect emphasizes the evil of its inhabitant because it is a door which suggests its owner doesn't care about how he appears to the world:

> The door, which was equipped with neither bell nor knocker, was blistered and distained. Tramps slouched into the recess and struck matches on the panels; children kept shop upon the steps; the schoolboy had tried his knife on the mouldings

In a sense it is true that Hyde doesn't care about appearances: he has made no attempt to mend the door because it is "blistered" and "disdained". This description works on a symbolic level because the door could symbolize Hyde's character, personality or soul: like the door there is something "blistered" about his being, he is mentally diseased. He certainly is "distained", which here carries a double meaning because it can mean "discoloured" or "disliked by people". Hyde doesn't care what people think of him, but Jekyll does. In stark contrast, Jekyll's door is well-kept and large. Here we see Utterson knocking on it:

> One house, however, second from the corner, was still occupied entire; and at the door of this, which wore a great

air of wealth and comfort, though it was now plunged in darkness except for the fanlight, Mr. Utterson stopped and knocked. A well-dressed, elderly servant opened the door.

The description of Jekyll's door is symbolic too because it suggests how Jekyll wants to appear to the world: with a "great air of wealth and comfort". However, we realize that the fact that it is "plunged in darkness" is significant too because Jekyll himself, we learn later, is plunged in the darkness of Hyde. Here then is a door which presents the public face of Jekyll to the world is there for everyone to see, while Hyde's door is hidden away in an alley where respectable people rarely go. Later on in the novel, doors become even more significant because it is the door which generates the mystery regarding the whereabouts of Jekyll. Poole is very upset when he says to Utterson in 'The Last Night':

> Do you think I do not know where his head comes to in the cabinet door, where I saw him every morning of my life?

Poole had seen "something" through the door and was able to judge the person's height by measuring it against the door; thus we see the door assisting him with the realisation that it is not Jekyll. The door here, as before, becomes another clue that something is terribly wrong. Poole also points out that the servants have had to deal with a "closed door" and not Jekyll for a week. The door is a symbol of Jekyll's secrecy and his desperation. Poole says to Utterson:

> We've had nothing else this week back; nothing but papers, and a closed door, and the very meals left there to be smuggled in when nobody was looking.

The opening of the door allows Jekyll/Hyde to eat and to survive, while the fact that it is shut upon his servants and friends symbolises Jekyll's "social death"; his inability to communicate properly with people and the world. Ultimately, the door to Jekyll's laboratory stands between Utterson and the truth of what has happened to Jekyll. The knocking down of this door is one of the great set-pieces of the novel, and again like the descriptions analysed above is symbolically significant; finally Jekyll's secret is being destroyed with the destruction of the door.

"Ah, that's not Jekyll's voice—it's Hyde's!" cried Utterson. "Down with the door, Poole!"

Poole swung the axe over his shoulder; the blow shook the building, and the red baize door leaped against the lock and hinges. A dismal screech, as of mere animal terror, rang from the cabinet. Up went the axe again, and again the panels crashed and the frame bounded; four times the blow fell; but the wood was tough and the fittings were of excellent workmanship; and it was not until the fifth, that the lock burst and the wreck of the door fell inwards on the carpet.

The door here is of "excellent workmanship" and its wood is "tough"; this could symbolize the power of Jekyll's disguise, the power of Hyde himself, because this strong, heavy door has stopped the world learning the truth about his terrible experiment.

Essay question
Discuss the symbolism of doors in this novel.

Possible essay plan
Introduction:
Discuss why doors can be viewed as a symbol in poetry and novels: they are often "openings" to other worlds, metaphors for change
Main body:
Discuss what Hyde's door symbolizes: his evil, his neglect and contempt for the world, his secrecy, his escape from blame
Discuss what Jekyll's door symbolizes: his respectability, his public face to the world
Discuss the symbolism of the "knocking down" of Jekyll's cabinet door, and how the door symbolizes Jekyll's destruction
Conclusion:
Sum up your findings; discuss how doors symbolize a few different ideas and themes in the novel

Fog and darkness

Stevenson uses descriptions of fog and darkness to great effect in the novel. Dickens had described the fog in London very famously at the beginning of *Bleak House* in order to evoke a decayed, anxious atmosphere. Stevenson uses fog in London to create an atmosphere of horror and claustrophobia. In 'Search for Mr Hyde' Utterson is described in this fashion:

> In the morning before office hours, at noon when business was plenty, and time scarce, at night under the face of the fogged city moon, by all lights and at all hours of solitude or concourse, the lawyer was to be found on his chosen post.

Here the fog isn't as bad as it becomes later on in the novel. Utterson is represented as a man who is determined to find the truth in the fog, braving it at all hours of the day. The fog here is used not so much as a symbol but to create the atmosphere of Utterson's lonely vigil. Later on though, the fog becomes more sinister. Just before the murder of Carew, the fog is described in this fashion:

> Although a fog rolled over the city in the small hours, the early part of the night was cloudless, and the lane, which the maid's window overlooked, was brilliantly lit by the full moon.

We have here a mixed picture of London: it is a beautiful, cloudless night, lit by the full moon. The atmosphere makes the maid think of romance and her loved one, but the fog gives the night a sinister tinge as does the full moon on reflection because this is, of course, when madness is at its height. The word "lunacy" comes from the Latin word for moon "luna": people believed that the full moon could cause madness. This is certainly what we see happening with Hyde who kills Carew for no good reason at all.

During the morning after the murder though, the atmosphere has changed completely. In one of the most horrifying descriptions in the novel, Stevenson writes:

> It was by this time about nine in the morning, and the first fog of the season. A great chocolate-coloured pall lowered over heaven, but the wind was continually charging and routing these embattled vapours; so that as the cab crawled from street to street, Mr. Utterson beheld a marvellous number of degrees and hues of twilight; for here it would be dark like the back-end of evening; and there would be a glow of a rich, lurid brown, like the light of some strange conflagration; and here, for a moment, the fog would be quite broken up, and a haggard shaft of daylight would glance in between the swirling wreaths.

Of all the descriptions in the novel, this description best reveals a literary device known as the "pathetic fallacy": this is when the weather reflects or mirrors the mood of a character or the story. This is certainly the case here: the wind is surging violently around the city, reflecting the violence of Hyde, while the daylight is described as "haggard", tired and ugly and defeated, which certainly reflects Utterson's mood, and is symbolic of his desperation to find a solution to the Jekyll/Hyde problem. But it is interesting to note that the darkness is "man-made" because the "chocolate-coloured pall" has almost certainly been created by the factories and chimneys in the city. The fact that this made-man smog is compared to a "pall" is important: a "pall" is the cloth put over a coffin during a funeral, thus suggesting that the city itself is a dead body with the pall thrown over it. Even though it is morning, it feels like the onset of night, or the "back-end of evening", with the streets revealing lots of different twilit colours. While this is a nightmarish vision of the city, it is a rather marvellous one: this is more like the city of a nightmare or bad dream than a real one. In such a way, we could speculate that the fog and darkness symbolises a few different things here: it symbolises Utterson's confusion and bewilderment, it symbolises the destructiveness of the modern city, it symbolises Hyde's evil intent, but it also symbolises the ghastly, dream-like wonder of Hyde.

Essay
Explore what the fog and darkness symbolise in this novel.

Possible plan
Introduction:
Discuss the ways in which fog and darkness can symbolise confusion and evil in various works of literature. Discuss the context of Stevenson's novel, and the fact that London and most cities were covered in industrial smogs, which were artificial fogs and created darkness during the day-time
Main body:
Discuss the way in which Stevenson uses fog and darkness early on in the novel to create a Gothic atmosphere, and that this fog lightly suggests mystery
Discuss how after the murder of Carew, the descriptions of darkness and fog in the morning are richly symbolic and work on many different levels. Analyse this passage in detail
Conclusion:

Sum up your points, showing that Stevenson uses fog as a motif to suggest the confusion of Utterson and the mystery and horror of Hyde as well as the "modern city".

The bogeyman

The novel was described by Stevenson as a "bogeyman" tale. In Hyde, Stevenson created the most horrifying "bogeyman" of all, the bogeyman that is within all of us: what we are like in our worst moments, a representation of our most despicable desires and hatreds. The idea of the novel began with Stevenson having a dream which was very similar to the one that he writes for Utterson in 'Search for Mr Hyde':

> The figure in these two phases haunted the lawyer all night; and if at any time he dozed over, it was but to see it glide more stealthily through sleeping houses, or move the more swiftly and still the more swiftly, even to dizziness, through wider labyrinths of lamplighted city, and at every street corner crush a child and leave her screaming. And still the figure had no face by which he might know it; even in his dreams, it had no face, or one that baffled **(confused)** and melted before his eyes;

The dream is truly nightmarish because it visualises two of our most common fears: that an adult would want to kill a child, and that a figure might be stalking over us while we are sleeping, which Utterson sees happening to Jekyll in his dream. To make matters even worse, the figure has no "face" and when he does catch sight of it, it "melts" before his eyes. The bogeyman then is both human and not-human: he is shadowy and evil, he seems to have super-human powers to be here, there and everywhere, and he catches people at their most vulnerable, either by picking on children or while we are asleep. This bogeyman is more than a ghost: he is a symbol of our deepest fears. Stevenson's skill as a novelist is to reveal that the bogeyman though is not a monster that exists outside us, but actually is part and parcel of who we are. Hyde behaves like a psychotic as we see in the murder of Carew, but he is not an "alien" from outer space, but more of a throw-back to our evolutionary ancestors, the apes:

And next moment, with ape-like fury, he was trampling his victim under foot and hailing down a storm of blows, under which the bones were audibly **(could be heard)** shattered and the body jumped upon the roadway.

The description of Hyde as "ape-like" is important, and is imagery that is sustained throughout the novel: Hyde is merely who we used to be, an "ape". He also is visibly child-like in this description: he stamps on Carew in the same way that a child might stamp on a toy, revelling in the sound of the toy shattering. This sense that Hyde symbolises our inner-most natures is heightened and explored in Jekyll's "Full Statement of the Case" when he recounts how he woke up one morning as Hyde:

But the hand which I now saw, clearly enough, in the yellow light of a mid-London morning, lying half shut on the bedclothes, was lean, corded, knuckly, of a dusky pallor (colour) and thickly shaded with a swart growth of hair. It was the hand of Edward Hyde.

Here Stevenson develops the "ape-like" imagery by describing Hyde's hand more or less as an "ape's" hand, one which is hairy, muscly, "corded" and dark. This is a murderer's hand, this is the bogeyman's hand, and it is actually Jekyll's, the supposedly respectable doctor who helps charitable causes.

Essay
Analyse the role that the "bogeyman" plays in this novel.

Possible plan
Introduction:
Discuss how Stevenson intended the novel to be a "bogeyman" tale, discuss why they were and are popular stories to write
Main body:
Discuss Utterson's dream, analysing the role of the bogeyman in it.
Discuss the representation of Hyde as being "ape-like", a psychotic, and child-like
Discuss why Stevenson made Jekyll and Hyde be the same person, and the implications of that
Conclusion:
Sum up your points, pointing out how the bogeyman is symbolic of our deepest fears that the bogeyman lurks within us

Expressions

Stevenson pays particular attention to how people look and make faces in this novel. His description of their expressions is a running "motif", a repeated pattern of images which are used to convey the personality and hidden natures of the characters. In this regard, he was probably influenced by some prominent criminologists of the day, such as Cesar Lombroso, who believed that you could work out whether someone was a criminal by the way they looked. This is certainly the case with both Hyde and Jekyll. Let's look at one of the first descriptions of Hyde, in 'Story of the Door'. Enfield describes Hyde in this way:

> there was the man in the middle, with a kind of black sneering coolness—frightened too, I could see that—but carrying it off, sir, really like Satan

The "black sneering coolness" is a suggestive description. The "black" is a manifestation of Hyde's evil, the darkness of his soul, the "sneering" reveals Hyde's contempt and dismissal of other people and their troubles, while the "coolness" suggests the way in which Hyde has no feelings of empathy. Hyde's looks are in marked contrast to Jekyll's, which are described here when Utterson brings up the matter of Hyde:

> The large handsome face of Dr. Jekyll grew pale to the very lips, and there came a blackness about his eyes. "I do not care to hear more," said he. "This is a matter I thought we had agreed to drop."

Jekyll is not ugly or deformed like Hyde, but has a "large handsome face": this suggests someone who is successful, wealthy, and high up on the evolutionary scale, a successful manifestation of the species. However, we see intimations of Hyde in the description of him when the name of Hyde is mentioned because a "blackness" comes about his eyes. This is the same blackness we saw when Hyde was challenged about trampling upon the little girl. Thus we can see that Stevenson is possibly challenging the thinkers of his day, such as Lombroso, who believed you could tell whether someone was a criminal by their physical features: Jekyll doesn't look like a criminal at all. However, at times, his expressions reveal his inner-most blackness; it is not his immediate looks that give him away, but his behaviour. Later on in the novel, after the murder of Carew, Jekyll's looks are described again in 'Incident at the Window'. Jekyll is sits talking to Enfield and Utterson from his window when this happens:

> "That is just what I was about to venture to propose," returned the doctor with a smile. But the words were hardly uttered, before the smile was struck out of his face and succeeded by an expression of such abject terror and despair, as froze the very blood of the two gentlemen below.

Jekyll's expression of "abject terror and despair" deeply affects Enfield and Utterson who are looking at him, freezing their blood. We realise later on that Jekyll is aware that he is about to turn into Hyde again and that he has no choice over the matter. The expression on his face reveals how powerless he is, and how he has become a victim of his own experiment. Stevenson uses the description of the expression to heighten both mystery and horror at this moment in the novel, as he has done before when he described Jekyll's "blackness about the eyes" because we never quite know why, at this point, Jekyll is looking this way.

In 'Remarkable Incident of Dr Lanyon', we learn about the change that has happened to Lanyon's looks:

> He had his death-warrant written legibly upon his face. The rosy man had grown pale; his flesh had fallen away; he was visibly balder and older; and yet it was not so much these tokens of a swift physical decay that arrested the lawyer's notice, as a look in the eye and quality of manner that seemed to testify to some deep-seated terror of the mind.

This description works because of the contrasts it makes between how Lanyon used to appear and how he appears now that he has learned the truth about Jekyll. His "rosy" or healthy complexion has become "pale", his "flesh had fallen away", his hair has fallen out and he looks older. However, as with Jekyll, it is not so much how he looks which is the most important thing but the way his eyes reveal a "deep-seated terror of the mind". This terror is in contrast to the blackness about Jekyll's eyes: Lanyon has seen Jekyll/Hyde's blackness and it has terrified him. He is in a worse state than Jekyll in the 'Incident of the Window'. Stevenson uses this description to heighten the mystery of the novel because at this point we don't know exactly what Lanyon knows. There is a real sense of pathos as well because it is terrible to see such a successful, happy man brought down so low. Thus, we, the reader, who had very little for the pompous Lanyon at the beginning of the novel, now do.

It is worth looking at the description which Jekyll gives when he first sees Hyde because his reaction to Hyde is quite different to other people:

> Again, in the course of my life, which had been, after all, nine tenths a life of effort, virtue and control, it had been much less exercised and much less exhausted. And hence, as I think, it came about that Edward Hyde was so much smaller, slighter and younger than Henry Jekyll. Even as good shone upon the countenance of the one, evil was written broadly and plainly on the face of the other. Evil besides (which I must still believe to be the lethal side of man) had left on that body an imprint of deformity and decay. And yet when I looked upon that ugly idol in the glass, I was conscious of no repugnance, rather of a leap of welcome. This, too, was I. It seemed natural and human. In my eyes it bore a livelier image of the spirit, it seemed more express and single, than the imperfect and divided countenance I had been hitherto accustomed to call mine. And in so far I was doubtless right. I have observed that when I wore the semblance of Edward Hyde, none could come near to me at first without a visible misgiving of the flesh. This, as I take it, was because all human beings, as we meet them, are commingled out of good and evil: and Edward Hyde, alone in the ranks of mankind, was pure evil.

It is fascinating to see that when Jekyll sees Hyde he feels not "repugnance" but a "leap of welcome". He realises that Hyde is "I". Jekyll knows that Hyde is ugly but thinks that Hyde reveals a "livelier image of the spirit", the face seems more "express" – i.e. quicker – and "single" – i.e. purposeful – than his face which was "imperfect" and "divided". In Jekyll's view his face conveys"dividedness"; it shows complexity while Hyde's face is "single" or simple in its purpose. There is no moral confusion about Hyde, he just feels that he can do what he wants, and this is what his ugly face reveals: the fact that he is "pure evil". So Hyde's face is an expression of Jekyll's inner evil. This, Jekyll explains, is why people have a "visible misgiving of the flesh" when they see Hyde.

Essay

Discuss the role that people's facial expressions play in the novel.

Possible plan

Introduction:

Discuss the context of the time and now and the reasons why people think they can see someone's inner character in a person's face and expressions.

Main body:

Discuss the descriptions of Hyde's expressions and facial characteristics, and why people feel uneasy around him. Discuss the symbolism of the blackness of his expression.

Discuss the descriptions of Jekyll's face and expressions.

Discuss Lanyon's change in appearance and how this creates sympathy for his character.

Conclusion:

Sum up your thoughts on the role that the descriptions of physical expressions play in the novel, showing that they are a running motif in the novel.

1 Story of the Door

YouTube reading:

http://www.youtube.com/watch?v=BMhePVqxdS8

Thematic questions

Who do you trust? Why do you trust them?

Are boring, quiet people like Utterson more trustworthy than exciting people?

What do "run-down" places tell us about the people who live there?

What are the most shocking things you have heard about?

Summary – fill in the blanks (answers are at the back)

Mr Utterson is a boring but "loveable" lawyer who people get help from when they are in ----. He is friends with a cousin, Enfield, and goes on regular walks with him on Sundays. One Sunday, they pass a dirty ---- in a poor area. Enfield tells Utterson a story about the door and the man who lives behind it. He says he saw a small, revolting man ------ -- a small --- of eight at 3am in the morning. A crowd, led by Enfield, confronted the man and forced him to pay --- in compensation. The man gave them a cheque which we learn at the very end of the chapter was signed by ----- ----, a very ----- person: no one believed that the cheque was ----- but later found out it was. Utterson is worried that Jekyll is being -------- by Mr Hyde.

Comprehension questions

What type of person is Utterson? Why do "downgoing men" seek him out?

Why do Enfield and Utterson go for a walk together every Sunday?

What was of interest about the door that Enfield tells the story about? What did it look like?

What did Enfield witness regarding Hyde and the small girl?

Why and how did the crowd manage to get Hyde to write the girl's family a cheque? What was odd about the cheque?

What is strange about Mr Hyde according to Enfield?

Analytical questions

Our first encounter with Hyde is an "eye-witness" account from Enfield. Why do you think Stevenson chose to introduce Hyde in this way?

What adjectives and imagery are used to describe Hyde?

Evaluative questions

How successful is this opening to the novel? Discuss the parts of the chapter that must have affected its first readers very deeply.

Creative response tasks

Imagine you are Utterson. Write his diary after this chapter has happened.

Write a story about a violent incident you have witnessed or have heard about that has affected you deeply.

You can watch some YouTube videos I made about this chapter of the book here:
Part One:
http://www.youtube.com/watch?v=PpOXi8PSwVI
Part Two:
http://www.youtube.com/watch?v=5UuF8-BYbHk
Part Three:
http://www.youtube.com/watch?v=tuTG95q9rSk

POSSIBLE ANSWERS in brief & bold

Comprehension questions

What type of person is Utterson? Why do "downgoing men" seek him out? **Utterson is a lawyer, and a loyal friend who can be trusted by respectable men who are in trouble or facing a scandal.**

Why do Enfield and Utterson go for a walk together every Sunday? **They are related and enjoyed each other's company even though they don't talk much.**

What was of interest about the door that Enfield tells the story about? What did it look like? **The door is very scruffy and dirty and in a poor area. It was the door that a violent man opened.**

What did Enfield witness regarding Hyde and the small girl? **Hyde trampled on a small girl of eight at three in the morning.**

Why and how did the crowd manage to get Hyde to write the girl's family a cheque? What was odd about the cheque? **The crowd told Hyde that they would make a "scandal" of the situation if he did not give the girl's family some money. The cheque was odd because it was signed by a very respectable man – who we later learn is Dr Jekyll.**

What is strange about Mr Hyde according to Enfield? **Hyde appears deformed in some sort of way, but it is difficult express why he is so unpleasant in words.**

Analytical questions

Our first encounter with Hyde is an "eye-witness" account from Enfield. Why do you think Stevenson chose to introduce Hyde in this way? **Stevenson's central aim at this section is to build up both a sense of mystery and horror regarding Hyde. The story is a very disturbing one because only a deeply unpleasant man would trample upon a girl of eight: this incident generates a real sense of horror regarding the character. The reader thinks** if Hyde can trample upon a girl of eight, then what else can he do? Stevenson also makes Hyde deeply mysterious in a number of ways, which also contributes to the suspense. Lots of unanswered questions come into the reader's mind: how and why is Hyde writing cheques signed by a respectable man? Why does he live in such a grotty place if he is wealthy? Why can no one describe him properly?

What adjectives and imagery are used to describe Hyde? **Hyde is described as "cool" and "ugly": both these adjectives have a disturbing effect upon the reader because of their context. Despite the fact that Hyde has just trampled on a small girl, he is "cool": in other words, he is not emotional or remorseful in any fashion. His physical appearance also makes him seem very unpleasant: he is "ugly" and there is a "strong feeling of deformity" about him. It is interesting to note that no one can describe exactly what he looks like. Enfield talks of him being a "damned Juggernaut": he seems to have superhuman powers and strength despite being so small.**

Evaluative questions

How successful is this opening to the novel? Discuss the parts of the chapter that most have affected its first readers very deeply. **The chapter is great at provoking the reader's curiosity in Hyde and his relationship with Dr Jekyll. Stevenson uses the figure of Utterson to create this curiosity: it is Utterson, Jekyll's friend, who guesses that there is a connection between the two men. Utterson's caring nature gives the story a sympathetic character, which is important.**

2 Search for Mr Hyde

YouTube reading:
http://www.youtube.com/watch?v=6L2GVGT7joU

Thematic questions

When and why do people become very interested in other people's lives? Why do people "spy" on each other?

When have you met someone you really don't like on first sight? Why did you not like them? What was it about their appearance that you didn't like?

Summary -- fill in the blanks (answers are at the back)

The lawyer Utterson is troubled by the --- that Henry Jekyll has written because it hands over everything to ----- --- if Jekyll dies or disappears for more than three months.

Utterson visits Dr. Lanyon, a friend of Jekyll's, to find out more, but discovers that Lanyon has ----- --- with Jekyll over the "unscientific" experiments Jekyll has been conducting. That night, Utterson suffers from nightmares. In one nightmare, he sees the figure of the man who trampled on the girl, and in another nightmare, the same figure approaches the sleeping Jekyll and makes Jekyll do what he wants. This figure has no ----. On waking, Utterson is determined to find out what Hyde looks like so he spends his spare time standing by the door where Hyde lives. Eventually, one night, Hyde arrives and Utterson asks to look at his face: Hyde shows him it and then gives Utterson his -----. Utterson realizes that Hyde is thinking about the will and is frightened for Jekyll. When he goes to visit Jekyll, we realize something Utterson has known for a while that the house that Hyde lives in is actually the laboratory attached to the back of Jekyll's house. Utterson finds that Jekyll is out, and learns from the butler, Poole, that Hyde has a --- to Jekyll's laboratory and the servants have orders to --- him. Utterson leaves feeling very worried that Hyde is blackmailing Jekyll.

Comprehension questions
Why is Utterson so upset about Jekyll's will?
Why does Utterson visit Lanyon? Why has Lanyon lost interest in Jekyll as a scientist?
What is Utterson worried about and what does he dream about?
What steps does Utterson take to find Mr Hyde?
Why does Hyde accuse Utterson of lying to him?
Why does Utterson visit Jekyll immediately after seeing Hyde?
Why is Utterson even more worried about Jekyll at the end of the chapter?
Analytical questions
How does Stevenson generate suspense in this chapter?
How does Stevenson create a Gothic atmosphere in his description of the streets of London and Utterson's dreams?
Evaluative questions
How successful is Stevenson in creating a mood of mystery in this chapter?
Creative response tasks
Write Utterson's diary entry for this chapter, detailing his encounters with Lanyon, with Mr Hyde, and his worries for Henry Jekyll.

Write a story or poem about a nightmare that comes true, calling it "Nightmare".

You can watch a YouTube video I made about this section of the book here:

POSSIBLE ANSWERS in brief & bold

Comprehension questions

Why is Utterson so upset about Jekyll's will? **Because he has left all his estate (money and property) to Hyde if he dies or disappears for more than three months.**
Why does Utterson visit Lanyon? Why has Lanyon lost interest in Jekyll as a scientist? **Utterson wants to find out why Lanyon has fallen out with Jekyll, and wants to know if it has anything to do with him knowing something unpleasant about Jekyll. However, he finds out, to his relief, that they have fallen out over a difference of opinion about science; Lanyon believes Jekyll is involved in "unscientific balderdash".**
What is Utterson worried about and what does he dream about? **He is very worried about his good friend Jekyll being blackmailed by Hyde, and possibly being harmed by him.**
What steps does Utterson take to find Mr Hyde? **Utterson waits by Hyde's door day and night.**
Why does Hyde accuse Utterson of lying to him? **Utterson says that Jekyll has told him about Hyde. Hyde knows this is a lie because of course Hyde is Jekyll, and Jekyll has, of course, said nothing about Hyde to Utterson.**
Why does Utterson visit Jekyll immediately after seeing Hyde? **First because Hyde's apartment is actually part of Jekyll's house: it is the back of Jekyll's very large house. This means it is easy for him to see Jekyll. Second because he is very worried about his friend being in trouble in some way.**
Why is Utterson even more worried about Jekyll at the end of the chapter? **He is extremely worried that Jekyll will come to harm; that Hyde will hurt Jekyll in some terrible way. Both his dream and his meeting with Hyde have persuaded him of this. Hyde's apparent interest in Utterson knowing where he lives has made Utterson think that Hyde knows about the will; since he now knows where Hyde lives, he will be more easily able to give the will to Hyde. He can see Hyde thinking this.**

Analytical questions

How does Stevenson generate suspense in this chapter? **Stevenson generates suspense by making Utterson look in such a determined way for Hyde: there is an element of a "hunt" here -- and a mystery. We really want to know what will happen when Utterson meets Hyde. When he does, the meeting is very tense: Hyde seems very anti-social except when he appears to be thinking about the will. This leads the reader to think that**

Hyde may well be planning for Jekyll to die soon so that he can inherit his money. **The reader thinks that maybe Hyde is planning Jekyll's murder. The dialogue between Utterson and Hyde is brief and tense. Stevenson's descriptions in the chapter are highly suspenseful: the description of the dreams Utterson has of the faceless figures are genuinely horrific and based on Stevenson's own dreams.**

How does Stevenson create a Gothic atmosphere in his description of the streets of London and Utterson's dreams? **The London that Stevenson describes is a "Gothic" London full of darkness and fog, which appears to be both literal and metaphorical. The characters in the novel are immersed in darkness or evil, and the fog could suggest their moral confusion as well.**

Evaluative questions

How successful is Stevenson in creating a mood of mystery in this chapter? **Stevenson's ability to tell a fascinating, fast-paced mystery story as well as his facility to describe London and Utterson's nightmares make this a highly successful chapter. Above all, it is his characterisation of Hyde which makes the story so gripping: Hyde is only shown in "little bursts" but what we do see is very disturbing. This is a man who appears capable of murder and even worse.**

3 Dr Jekyll was quite at ease

YouTube reading:

http://www.youtube.com/watch?v=poBMLbgXOWs

Thematic questions

What makes someone a "pedant" – a person who nit-picks over tiny details? Do you know any pedants? What are they like?

Do you know anyone who has had friends who have been a "bad influence"? What was the situation?

Has anyone made you promise anything that you have felt uncomfortable about?

Summary -- fill in the blanks (answers are at the back)

A fortnight (two weeks) later, Jekyll has a ---- party. Utterson remains behind so that he can speak to Jekyll about why he doesn't like Jekyll's will; he tells Jekyll that he can be ---- and urges Jekyll to tell him if he is being -------. Jekyll tells him that it isn't blackmail and that he can get rid of -- ---- at any time he wishes. He asks Utterson to drop the matter and make sure that he will help Hyde get what is in the will – i.e. everything Jekyll owns -- if he, Jekyll, ----- or ---.

Comprehension questions
Why does Jekyll think Lanyon is a pedant?
What does Jekyll make Utterson promise? Why is Utterson uneasy about the promise?
What is Jekyll's state of mind at this point do you think?

Analytical questions
How does Stevenson present Jekyll in this chapter? How does he create a sense of mystery around the character?

Evaluative questions
How successful is Stevenson in creating a sense of mystery in this chapter?

Creative response tasks
Write a story or poem about a friend who is a good person but befriends a bully who is a bad influence, calling the story "Bad Influence".

Write Utterson's diary for this chapter.

POSSIBLE ANSWERS in brief & bold

Comprehension questions
Why does Jekyll think Lanyon is a pedant? **Jekyll thinks that Lanyon is "nit-picking" when he criticises Jekyll's scientific experiments and ideas.**
What does Jekyll make Utterson promise? Why is Utterson uneasy about the promise? **He makes him promise that he will do his best for Hyde if he dies or disappears: in other words make sure Hyde enjoys the contents of the will. Utterson does not like Hyde and is worried that Jekyll may be murdered by Hyde in order to get the contents of the will.**
What is Jekyll's state of mind at this point do you think? **On the surface, Jekyll appears to be "normal" in that he is socialising and seeing people. However, the moment that Utterson questions him about Hyde a "paleness comes to his lips and blackness about the eyes". He is obviously very worried in some kind of way about Hyde, but won't explain exactly what his worries are.**

Analytical questions
How does Stevenson present Jekyll in this chapter? How does he create a sense of mystery around the character? **Stevenson presents Jekyll as someone who appears on the surface to be happy, but clearly is in a disturbed state of mind deep down. We see how unnerved he becomes when he is asked about Hyde: he becomes "pale"**

and there is"blackness about his eyes". The description of the "blackness" is interesting because it suggests a much darker side to Jekyll. When we hear about Jekyll saying that he has a great interest in Hyde, we feel rather sickened because we know that Jekyll is friends with a man who trampled on a little girl. And we are fascinated too: what hold does Hyde have over Jekyll?

Evaluative questions

How successful is Stevenson in creating a sense of mystery in this chapter? **The mystery is generated by the reader trying to guess the relationship between Hyde and Jekyll. Even when we know the solution to the mystery, the book is enjoyable to re-read because we see more clearly just how "conflicted" Jekyll is about Hyde. He is clearly pleased to have a friend who he can get rid of at any time, but he is also worried that Hyde may take over him: this is why he has written the will. The pleasure in reading the book for the first time is the pleasure in trying to find out the mystery; the pleasure on second reading is the pleasure of working out Jekyll's complex psychological relationship with his "dark side", with his Mr Hyde.**

4 The Carew Murder Case

YouTube reading:
http://www.youtube.com/watch?v=tbNXB3wdHAw
Thematic questions

Why do you think people commit murder? What types of people commit murder? Are they inherently evil or has something in their past life "led them astray"?
Why do thugs assault people in the street? What makes them do this?

Summary -- fill in the blanks (answers are at the back)

A year later, a maid is sitting at her window during the early hours of the morning when she witnesses Mr Hyde, someone she knows, beat a polite, old gentleman to ---- with a stick, which ----. She faints and then when she wakes up contacts the police who find a letter addressed to--- ---- on the old man. Called on early that morning by the police, Utterson identifies the body at the police station as Sir Danvers Carew, one of his ----. Utterson then recognizes the broken stick as ----- ----. Inspector Newcomen and he visit Hyde's run-down flat and find the ----- ---- there, and a burnt ----. The inspector believes that all they have to do is wait at the --- for Hyde to draw out money because he has no way getting any otherwise. However, Hyde wasn't --- again.

Comprehension questions
What were the circumstances of the murder of Sir Danvers Carew? How was he killed?
Why was Utterson contacted?
What incriminating evidence was found in Hyde's rooms?
Why is Hyde now a hunted man?
Analytical questions
How does Stevenson convey a sense of horror and mystery in this chapter?
Look at Stevenson's descriptions of London and Hyde's flat: how does he generate a Gothic atmosphere here?
Evaluative questions
How successful is Stevenson in making Hyde seem genuinely evil?
Creative response tasks
Write the newspaper article about the murder of Carew.

Continue Utterson's diary for this chapter of the novel, detailing his thoughts on the murder and his discovery of the incriminating evidence in Jekyll's flat.

Write a story or poem called "The Murder".

You can watch a YouTube video I made about the chapter here:
http://www.youtube.com/watch?v=sk5jBmSVn_8

POSSIBLE ANSWERS in brief & bold

Comprehension questions
What were the circumstances of the murder of Sir Danvers Carew? How was he killed? **He was killed in October on a night which was cloudless and there was a full moon. Mr Hyde approached Sir Danvers Carew, exchanged a few words, which did not seem very important, and then lost his temper, clubbing the kind old man to death. He hit him so hard that the maid who witnessed the attack heard the old man's bones shatter. After witnessing the attack, the maid fainted and woke up at 2am, when she saw Hyde's broken stick lying near the old man. It was then that she contacted the police.**
Why was Utterson contacted? **Utterson was approached because when Sir Danver's clothes were searched, a letter addressed to him was found: Utterson was Sir Danver's lawyer.**

What incriminating evidence was found in Hyde's rooms? **The other half of the broken stick.**

Why is Hyde now a hunted man? **Because he murdered a very important politician, Sir Danvers Carew. Notice how people were less bothered about finding him after the attack on the girl, possibly because she was of a lower class than Sir Danvers.**

Analytical questions

How does Stevenson convey a sense of horror and mystery in this chapter? **Stevenson takes great care in describing the murder of Sir Danvers in a number of different ways. First, it is important that a maid witnesses the murder: she is an innocent by-stander and this gives her description more poignancy. Second, she knows Hyde: we never learn why, but this adds to a sense of mystery and menace about Hyde: maybe he has been attacking maids? Third, the maid's description is genuinely horrific: it appears that Hyde has attacked a man who described as being very "kindly" and "beautiful" with "white hair" for what appears to be no reason at all. The metaphor used to describe his anger is effective; the maid describes how he broke out in a "great flame of anger". This suggests both the power and horror of Hyde: he is a man who burns with anger. He is genuinely psychotic. Then Sir Danvers' bones are described as "audibly" shattering: in other words, the maid heard his bones crunch as he was smashed by Hyde's stick, which breaks from the violence of the attack.**

Look at Stevenson's descriptions of London and Hyde's flat: how does he generate a Gothic atmosphere here? **Stevenson creates a very Gothic atmosphere firstly by his descriptions of the fog and the darkness. Even though it is the morning, there is still darkness which is created by the fog: "a great chocolate-coloured pall" covers the whole of the city. This metaphor is particularly effective because a "pall" is a cloth spread over a coffin. In other words, it feels like the city itself is a coffin, which contains the dead body of the people. The daylight is described as "haggard": tired, wearied and ugly. Women who have their own "keys" wander about the area where Hyde lives: in Stevenson's day, women who had their own keys were probably prostitutes. The area has a "gin palace": this was a place to get very cheap, strong alcohol. "Ragged" children, who are probably homeless, "huddle in the doorways". This is a city of your worst nightmares: full of vice, of poverty, of unfairness, soaked in fog and a feeling of death.**

Evaluative questions

How successful is Stevenson in making Hyde seem genuinely evil?

Hyde's evil is evoked by the way he murders Carew. He appears to have murdered him for absolutely no reason at all. He is a man consumed by evil, which burns like a "great flame" within him. He seems to enjoy "trampling" upon people: this is a particularly cowardly method of attack. He only seems to pick upon people weaker than himself and seems to enjoy murdering Carew. He is a sadist: he enjoys seeing people suffer. Thus we can see that Stevenson is extremely successful in evoking Hyde's evil nature: we see him doing very evil things, and what is more we see him enjoying his evil deeds. He appears totally out of control. For me, his real evil comes from the fact that he only picks on weak people: he is a psychotic bully.

5 Incident of the letter

YouTube reading:
http://www.youtube.com/watch?v=BvinrLUD47Q
Thematic questions
When have you seen a friend or relative in distress? How you know the cause of their distress?
When has a friend tried to reassure you that they are fine when they are not?
When have you lied or been lied to?
Have you know anyone who has forged a note/letter, or pretended to be someone else? Why do you think people pretend to be other people?

Summary -- fill in the blanks (answers are at the back)
Utterson visits Henry Jekyll who, looking ---- ---, tells him that he has finished with ----. He shows Utterson a letter written by Hyde which says that Hyde has ---- and won't be caught. Hyde says that he is ---- of Jekyll's generosity. Utterson is pleased to read the letter, but then learns from Poole the butler that no one has delivered a ---- to the house. He shows the letter to a -------- expert, Mr Guest, who says that the letter is written in Jekyll's hand-writing, only the slope of the writing is different. Utterson is horrified that Jekyll would ---- a letter for a murderer.

Comprehension questions
What does the state of Jekyll's laboratory tell us about his state of mind?
What does the letter to Jekyll from Hyde say?
Why does Utterson believe Jekyll forged the letter?
Analytical questions

How does Stevenson reveal Jekyll's state of mind in this chapter? Think about his use of dialogue, the descriptions of the laboratory, and the plot twist that the letter is a forgery.

Evaluative questions

How successful is Stevenson in generating mystery and suspense in the chapter?

Creative response tasks

Write a story or poem called "The Forgery".

Write Utterson's diary for this chapter, discussing his feelings about seeing his friend Henry Jekyll and his concern when he finds out the letter is a forgery.

You can watch a YouTube video I made about this section here: http://www.youtube.com/watch?v=AS7-NztAoTk

POSSIBLE ANSWERS in brief & bold

Comprehension questions

What does the state of Jekyll's laboratory tell us about his state of mind? **That he is neglectful of his previous interests: all of his scientific equipment is unused. This suggests he is probably depressed because he is not pursuing his favourite past-time: science.**

What does the letter to Jekyll from Hyde say? **Hyde says that he has escaped and can't be caught, and that he will not return.**

Why does Utterson believe Jekyll forged the letter? **First, he learns from a servant that no one delivered the letter. Second, his friend Mr Guest, who is a hand-writing expert, notices that Hyde's handwriting in the letter is identical to Jekyll's, except that it is differently sloped.**

Analytical questions

How does Stevenson reveal Jekyll's state of mind in this chapter? Think about his use of dialogue, the descriptions of the laboratory, and the plot twist that the letter is a forgery. **Through his description of the abandoned and disused laboratory, he reveals that Jekyll is no longer pursing his passion, science, this suggests that Jekyll is depressed. When he talks to Jekyll, it is obvious that he is in a state of shock, but convinced that Hyde won't trouble him again. Stevenson's use of dialogue is effective in conveying Jekyll's sense of shock. However, the revelation that Jekyll has possibly forged the letter suggests that Jekyll is deceitful for some reason. This narrative "twist" is very effective in making the reader think that Jekyll is hiding some terrible secret, and is not to be trusted.**

Evaluative questions

How successful is Stevenson in generating mystery and suspense in the chapter? **Stevenson's characterisation of Jekyll as a cunning but shocked person is highly effective for a number of reasons. First, it creates mystery: we, as readers, are desperate to know the solution to the mystery. Second, it is highly successful in constructing a picture of a highly complex personality: Jekyll is not a "straight-forward" person at all, and this provokes our interest in the story further.**

6 Remarkable Incident of Dr Lanyon

YouTube reading:

http://www.youtube.com/watch?v=ypCi_vCJjrU

Thematic questions

Have you ever been in shock? What has happened to you?

Have you ever seen anyone in shock?

Have you ever met anyone who has changed a great deal since when you first met them? What was your reaction?

Summary -- fill in the blanks (answers are at the back)

Time passes but Hyde is not ----. Jekyll starts seeing people, doing --- works and holds a dinner party which ---- and ---- come to. A few days later though, when Utterson calls, Jekyll won't see ----. Utterson visits Lanyon and sees that Lanyon is sick and will --- soon. Lanyon won't talk about Jekyll, who he regards as ----. Utterson writes to Jekyll to ---- about not seeing him. Jekyll writes back and telling him that he does not blame Lanyon for treating him in this way and that he has brought a ---- upon himself. A few weeks later Lanyon dies, giving Utterson an envelope. When he opens it, he finds another envelope only to be opened ---- Jekyll disappears or dies. Utterson tries to see Jekyll again, but the butler ---- to let him in.

Comprehension questions

Dr Jekyll enters a new phase of life at the beginning of the chapter: what does he do that was different from before?

Then he refuses to see Utterson: why do you think – look at "Henry Jekyll's full statement of the case" for the answer?

How has Lanyon changed when Utterson visits him?
What letter does Utterson receive from Lanyon and what instructions come with it?

Analytical questions
How does Stevenson develop Lanyon's character in this chapter?

Evaluative questions
How successfully does Stevenson arouse the reader's curiosity in this chapter?

Creative response tasks
Write Utterson's diary for this chapter, explaining what he thinks and feels at Jekyll and Lanyon's behaviour.

Stevenson writes of Hyde at the beginning of the chapter: "Much of his past was unearthed, indeed, and all disreputable **(disgraceful/creating a poor reputation)**: tales came out of the man's cruelty, at once so callous and violent; of his vile life, of his strange associates **(people he knew)**, of the hatred that seemed to have surrounded his career". Write a series of newspaper articles about what Hyde has done.

Write a poem or story called "The Shock".

You can watch a YouTube video I made about this section here:
http://www.youtube.com/watch?v=VDO-vorkfUc

POSSIBLE ANSWERS in brief & bold

Comprehension questions
Dr Jekyll enters a new phase of life at the beginning of the chapter: what does he do that was different from before? **He does "good", i.e. charitable works. He also socialises like he used to, inviting Utterson and Lanyon to dinner.**
Then he refuses to see Utterson: why do you think – look at "Henry Jekyll's full statement of the case" for the answer? **We learn in Jekyll's narrative that he has been turning into Hyde without wishing to: this is the reason that he won't see anyone.**
How has Lanyon changed when Utterson visits him? **He has his "death warrant" written on his face, in other words, he is going to die.**
What letter does Utterson receive from Lanyon and what instructions come with it? **He receives a letter addressed to him but he is told that he must not open it until Jekyll has disappeared or died.**

Analytical questions
How does Stevenson develop Lanyon's character in this chapter? **Stevenson has been very careful to "develop" his characterisation of Lanyon in this chapter because he reveals him to be a very different man from the beginning of the book, where Lanyon was presented as a smug person who was**

utterly confident that Jekyll was pursuing "unscientific balderdash" and would have nothing to do with him and his projects. He was certain of himself and his views. In this chapter, we see a man who has had all of his views about life shattered and changed: he has lost his confidence and is about to die. He has changed very dramatically.

Evaluative questions
How successfully does Stevenson arouse the reader's curiosity in this chapter? **The change in Lanyon provokes the reader's curiosity because it is so extreme. We, as readers, wonder: how can such a confident and successful man change so dramatically? What has happened to cause his death?**

7 Incident at the window

YouTube reading:
http://www.youtube.com/watch?v=oc7Y7uwntgw
Thematic questions
Are there times when you find it difficult to talk to people and you'd prefer to be alone?
What kinds of people like to be alone and away from other people? Why are they this way?

Summary
Utterson and Enfield pass by the door where Enfield saw Hyde --- after he trampled the girl. Enfield has now worked out that it is the door to the laboratory that connects to ---- house. Enfield says that they will never --- Hyde again. They look up and see Jekyll at the window looking very ----. They ask him to come out for a ---- with them but he says he can't. Then a look of --- seizes him and he disappears. The two men walk on in ----.

Comprehension questions
What does Enfield discover about Hyde's rooms that he didn't know? Why do you think Utterson hadn't already told him this information? What are Jekyll's mood and emotions like in this chapter?
Analytical questions
How does Stevenson use description and dialogue to create a sense of drama and impending doom in this chapter?
Evaluative questions
How successful is this chapter in provoking the reader's curiosity?
Creative response tasks

Write a poem or short story about a brief but chilling meeting with a friend who is in a bad way, calling it "My Sad Friend".

Write Enfield's diary for this chapter in which he talks about his friendship with Utterson and his thoughts on Jekyll and Hyde.

You can watch a YouTube video I made about this section here:
http://www.youtube.com/watch?v=VDO-vorkfUc

POSSIBLE ANSWERS in brief & bold

Comprehension questions
What does Enfield discover about Hyde's rooms that he didn't know? **He realises that Hyde's living quarters are actually the back part of Dr Jekyll's house.**
Why do you think Utterson hadn't already told him this information? **Utterson is a very "discreet" person: he does not reveal his friend's secrets or troubles to anyone. Thus we see him as someone who can be trusted and doesn't gossip.**
What are Jekyll's mood and emotions like in this chapter? **Jekyll is revealed as being in a state of "abject terror" when he finishes talking to Enfield and Utterson: he is terrified in the most extreme fashion.**

Analytical questions
How does Stevenson use description and dialogue to create a sense of drama and impending doom in this chapter? **The description of Jekyll sitting in such a dejected way at the window creates a sense of impending doom because we see that hhe feels that he has no future prospects. He appears to be without hope: he can't even go out for a walk with his friends. Then when his mood shifts from one of depression to "abject terror" we have a sense that something terrible is going to happen to Jekyll.**

Evaluative questions
How successful is this chapter in provoking the reader's curiosity? **Stevenson's manages to carry on creating a deep and profound of mystery in this chapter because, on first reading, we don't know what is troubling Jekyll or what is making his mood swing so sharply. As far as we are concerned, Hyde has disappeared and therefore Jekyll possibly doesn't need to worry about him. The shift from depression to "abject terror" is particularly perplexing. Why has he suddenly shut the window on his friends? What has happened to him to make him suddenly feel this way? The chapter, like the previous one, provokes many questions in the reader's mind.**

8 The Last Night

YouTube readings:
Part One: http://www.youtube.com/watch?v=RnTusZVnZNs
Part Two: http://www.youtube.com/watch?v=aGQakr19q8w

Thematic questions
What are the major confrontations you have had in your life?
Has there ever been a time when you have had to confront a friend or relative over their behavior? If so, what happened? If not, think about why some people encounter these times in their lives?

Summary -- fill in the blanks (answers are at the back)

One evening Utterson is visited by Poole who tells Utterson that he thinks there has been some "--- ---" regarding Dr Jekyll. Utterson goes with Poole to Jekyll's house and finds all the servants cowering in the ----. Poole and Utterson go quietly through the laboratory to the "cabinet" or small room where they knock. A ---- voice says that he cannot see anyone. Poole then tells him that he thinks Jekyll was "---- ---- ----" eight days before, and that the strange voice has spent much time demanding drugs, the orders for which are written on pieces of paper and pushed under the door. Utterson reads one of these notes, and thinks that Jekyll is ---. Poole then tells him that he has caught a glimpse of the "thing" and saw it was much --- than Jekyll. Utterson decides to break down the door and send two servants around the back to stop Hyde escaping. Utterson says to the creature in the laboratory that he will break down the door if Jekyll doesn't open it, to which a strange voice says "---- ---- !". When they break down the door, they find Hyde is ---- in Jekyll's large clothes and has just ---- himself by drinking poison. They find no sign of ----. On the business table, they find a will the same as the one that Jekyll wrote for Hyde except that ------ name has replaced Hyde's, and they find a note that asks Utterson to read ----- account and another letter, which is the "------" of Henry Jekyll.

Comprehension questions
Why does Poole ask for help? What is his mood?
What is the weather like?
Why are all the servants afraid?
What has Poole had to do for his master during these past few weeks?
What do Jekyll's notes to the chemist reveal about his state of mind?

What has Jekyll being doing these past few weeks? Why does Poole call him "it"?

Why and how do they break down the door?

When they break into the "cabinet" what do they find?

What evidence is there that Hyde has killed himself?

What evidence is there that Jekyll has been there very recently?

Analytical questions

How and why does Stevenson use the "pathetic fallacy" in this chapter?

How does Stevenson make this chapter so dramatic and yet manages to prolong the mystery?

Evaluative questions

How successful is Stevenson is creating an atmosphere of horror?

Creative response tasks

Write a story or poem called "The Disappearance" in which you describe the room of someone who has disappeared.

Write Poole's diary entry for this chapter, and other chapters where relevant. In the diary, get Poole to describe his relationship with Jekyll and his thoughts about his master.

You can watch a YouTube video I made about this section here:
http://www.youtube.com/watch?v=HQMt54K_vgw

POSSIBLE ANSWERS in brief & bold

Comprehension questions

Why does Poole ask for help? What is his mood? **He asks for help from Utterson because he suspects that there has been "foul play": he is very worried for the safety of his master.**

What is the weather like? **It is a clear night with a full moon and "diaphanous" or transparent clouds. It is very windy.**

Why are all the servants afraid? **They think something terrible has happened to Dr Jekyll and don't know what to do.**

What has Poole had to do for his master during these past few weeks? **He has had to take notes to the chemist which demand drugs which are "pure".**

What do Jekyll's notes to the chemist reveal about his state of mind? **He shows that he is very agitated because he has scribbled on the notes that he must have pure drugs using the phrase "for God's sake" in wild handwriting.**

What has Jekyll being doing these past few weeks? Why does Poole call him "it"? **Jekyll has shut himself away and won't see anyone, even his servants. Poole believes that Jekyll has been "made away with" – either kidnapped or killed – and that Hyde, who he calls "it", is living there.**

Why and how do they break down the door? **They believe Jekyll has been murdered. They break down the door with an axe.**

When they break into the "cabinet" what do they find? **They find a very "normal" or commonplace set up: a kettle on the oven, a fire in the grate, and papers on a business desk. The only strange thing initially they see are the chemicals in their "presses". Then they discover the dead body of Hyde in the larger clothes of Jekyll, twitching in the last throes of life.**
What evidence is there that Hyde has killed himself? **There is a "crush phial" in his hand which has contained poison.**
What evidence is there that Jekyll has been there very recently? **They find a letter written by him that day.**

Analytical questions

How and why does Stevenson use the "pathetic fallacy" in this chapter?
The wind is very "wild" and strong and it is a clear night with a full moon: the wind possibly could suggest the violence of Edward Hyde.
How does Stevenson make this chapter so dramatic and yet manages to prolong the mystery? **The chapter is punctuated by a number of gripping incidents. First, Poole's appearance at Utterson's door is dramatic because it is so unusual for the butler to leave Jekyll's house without his master's permission. The story he tells is wild and incomplete: he says that there has been "foul play" but we don't know exactly what "foul play" there has been. The reader begins to wonder whether Jekyll has been murdered or kidnapped by Hyde? Poole's mood adds to the tension: he is clearly in a state of near panic, which is unusual for this butler who is normally so calm. Second, Stevenson's descriptions of the places and the weather add to the dramatic tension because he describes a clear windy night with a full moon: this setting suggests that something supernatural is afoot. Other descriptions of the house, the laboratory and Jekyll's quiet room with the dead body of Hyde in it are very evocative. They provoke many questions which don't have answers: why is Hyde dead and not Jekyll? Stevenson's description of the servants huddled in the doorway adds to the sense of crisis and bemusement: why are they so frightened? Why don't they know what is going on? Then, Stevenson piles on the mystery when we listen to Poole's full explanation: he believes that Jekyll has been murdered by Hyde, but we wonder how the notes to the chemist, written in Jekyll's hand, have been written. Further tension is created by the strange, strangulated sound of Jekyll's voice pleading with Utterson to leave him alone. Stevenson's description of the breaking down of the door is incredibly powerful: he describes the violence with which Poole attacks the door in vivid imagery, deploying dynamic verbs to evoke a sense of violence. The door "leapt" off its hinges: this personification of the door adds to the sense**

of drama; even the door is in shock! Then the ensuing description of the quiet laboratory and the small body of Hyde twitching in the big clothes of Jekyll provide a nice contrast to the violence of the attack on the door. There is something horrifying and pitiable about the description of Hyde's body twitching in the huge clothes of Jekyll. It is also deeply mysterious: how and why has this happened? The mystery is furthered when we learn about the will being made out to Utterson and the fact that Jekyll himself is nowhere to be seen.

Evaluative questions
How successful is Stevenson is creating an atmosphere of horror? **The horror is generated not by description of lots of "blood and gore" but by the fact that we begin to realise that something truly terrifying has happened to both Hyde and Jekyll. Hyde who had seemed so indestructible is now lying dead in the huge clothes of Jekyll. Further horror is generated by the servants' reactions to Hyde and Jekyll: Poole, normally so calm, is in a state of total panic, while the other servants seemed to have completely imploded, huddling as they do in the doorway. Stevenson is successful in creating a sense of horror in the way he develops the mystery and forces us to think so hard about what has happened to Jekyll. The horror comes from us thinking about how this once respected man, who was so in command of his life, has been brought down so low: demanding drugs all the time and falling victim to the machinations of Hyde.**

9 Dr Lanyon's narrative

YouTube reading:
http://www.youtube.com/watch?v=iciliuhdvkA
Thematic questions
Think carefully about the topic of "transformation". Draw a spider-diagram of all the films/books/times where there is an interesting transformation, e.g. men turning into werewolves, people dressing up, changes in mood and personality. Why do you think "transformation" is such a major theme in this book and other texts?
Think about the times when you have had your beliefs changed or challenged. Why and how did it happen? Think about people like religious people/scientists who change their opinions, e.g. lose their faith/gain faith.

Summary -- fill in the blanks (answers are at the back)

Dr Lanyon talks about how he received a letter from Jekyll telling him to take a specific ---- from his laboratory and return to his house, where a man using Jekyll's name will come and collect the ----. Lanyon does as he was told, and meets at ---- a nasty little man at his door who comes into the laboratory and says that either Lanyon can ---- him take the drug, or not. If he does, he will see something that will "stagger the unbelief of ----". Lanyon then watches Hyde take the drug and turn into ----. He realises that Jekyll is ---- and that he ---- Carew. "The ----- ----" now afflicts him day and night.

Comprehension questions
What does Jekyll's letter to Lanyon order him to do?
What is Lanyon's reaction to Jekyll's letter and the contents of Jekyll's drawer?
What does Lanyon think of Hyde?
Why does Hyde warn Lanyon about if he watches him taking the potion?
What happens to Hyde and why is Lanyon so shocked? Why does the sight of Hyde's transformation cause his death?

Analytical questions
Why is this chapter written in the first person with Lanyon narrating?
How does Stevenson create a sense of drama when Hyde turns into Jekyll? How and why have many writers and film-makers imitated and borrowed from this scene?

Evaluative questions
We learn the answer to the mystery in this chapter. Do you think it is a good solution?

Creative response tasks
Write a story or poem called "The Transformation".

Write Utterson's diary in response to reading this account, discussing his feelings when he learns that Hyde is Jekyll. Is he as shocked as Lanyon?

POSSIBLE ANSWERS in brief & bold

Comprehension questions
What does Jekyll's letter to Lanyon order him to do? **He orders Lanyon to go to his room, or "cabinet", and collect some drugs from a specific drawer, and then return to his house where a man at midnight will collect the drugs for Jekyll.**
What is Lanyon's reaction to Jekyll's letter and the contents of Jekyll's drawer? **Lanyon thinks that Jekyll has probably lost his mind, that he has a "cerebral" or "brain" disease. He decides to arm**

himself with a revolver to defend himself. **He assumes that Jekyll must have lost his mind because of some experiment that has gone wrong: Lanyon is not surprised by this because he has always been suspicious of Jekyll's scientific methods.**
What does Lanyon think of Hyde? **Lanyon finds Hyde unpleasant but also ridiculous because he is dressed in clothes that are far too big for him. He notices that Hyde has a physical effect upon him, making him feel revolted.**
Why does Hyde warn Lanyon about watching him take the potion? **Because what Lanyon will see will "stagger the unbelief of Satan", in other words even the Devil himself would be amazed to see what he is going to see.**
What happens to Hyde and why is Lanyon so shocked? Why does the sight of Hyde's transformation cause his death? **Hyde turns into Jekyll. Lanyon is shocked for two reasons. First, because the transformation proves that Jekyll is a good scientist: he had called what Jekyll did previously "unscientific balderdash". Second, his faith in human nature is shaken: how could someone as respectable as Jekyll change into someone as evil as Hyde?**

Analytical questions

Why is this chapter written in the first person with Lanyon narrating? **Stevenson uses a number of different styles of writing in the book. The first half of the book is largely written in the third person, and is mainly a description of Utterson's quest to help his friend, Jekyll, and discover what his problems really are. The third person narrative style suits the "detective" genre of the writing. However, by having Lanyon tell his story in his own words makes the story all the more believable and emotional. We, the reader, become Lanyon himself as he watches Hyde transform into Jekyll: the first person narration allows us to feel his shock and pain at seeing his friend turn from the monster Hyde into his friend Henry Jekyll.**
How does Stevenson create a sense of drama when Hyde turns into Jekyll? How and why have many writers and film-makers imitated and borrowed from this scene? **Stevenson uses a great deal of "visual imagery" at key points in the book. Certain important scenes are described in so much detail that we can clearly visualise exactly what is happening. This is particularly the case with the transformation from Hyde to Jekyll.**

He put the glass to his lips and drank at one gulp. A cry followed; he reeled, staggered, clutched at the table and held on, staring with injected eyes, gasping with open mouth; and as I looked there came, I thought, a change—he seemed to swell—his face became suddenly black and the features seemed to melt and alter—and the next moment, I had sprung to my feet and leaped back against the wall, my arms raised to shield me from that prodigy, my mind submerged **(covered)** in terror.

"O God!" I screamed, and "O God!" again and again; for there before my eyes—pale and shaken, and half fainting, and groping before him with his hands, like a man restored from death—there stood Henry Jekyll!

We see here how Stevenson uses some very powerful verbs to describe the way in which Hyde is affected by drinking the potion: he "reels", "staggers", "clutches", "stares", "gasps". The effect of these verbs is to give the prose a real sense of action: each verb generates a visual image which suggests the pain of Jekyll. We see Hyde "staggering" around like someone who is drunk and has lost his faculty to stand properly; the verb "gasp" suggests that he is suffocating. In the next part, the verbs acquire a psychedelic, magical quality, Hyde's face "melts" and "alters": this is very sinister and possibly horrific to see someone's face melt like wax. Lanyon's reaction adds to the terror: he screams out "O God!" because he has no other response than this. What he is seeing is almost beyond words to convey.

Evaluative questions

We learn the answer to the mystery in this chapter. Do you think it is a good solution? **Some critics believe that the genius of the book is the solution to the mystery, which is both unexpected but obvious. Even when the novel is re-read again and again, it is this solution which intrigues, teases and attracts the reader: this horror story becomes a study of the human condition because of this solution. If Hyde had been another person or a ghost or ghoul, it would have been an ordinary ghost story about an evil person or thing who is the "shadow" of a good man. However, by making Jekyll and Hyde one and the same person, we begin to examine ourselves: do we not too have a "Hyde" within us? What would we do if we could have a Hyde who could do whatever he/she wanted without ever being caught? The novel thus moves from being a mystery story to a psychological fable which makes the reader ask questions of him or herself. Thus we could say the true horror of the story is that Stevenson has a point which is still true today: all of us have a "Hyde" within us. It comes as no surprise that the phrase a "Jekyll/Hyde character" has entered the language meaning a person who can suddenly switch from being very nice to committing evil.**

10 Henry Jekyll's full statement of the case

YouTube reading:

http://www.youtube.com/watch?v=16XShukmDEE

Thematic questions

If you knew you could "get away" with any crime you wanted, what crimes might you commit? What do you think other people would do in other circumstances?

Do you think human beings are both good and evil? Do you think they have two sides to their natures?

Are humans born good or evil, or do they learn to be that way?

Do humans have many different "personalities", more than two sides, depending upon the situations they are in?

Do you think that stopping people having what they want leads to them wanting it more?

Summary -- fill in the blanks (answers are at the back)

Jekyll talks about how he has since an early age two sides to his nature: the --- and the ---. When he became a scientist he became obsessed by how to separate these two elements of the human soul until one night he made a mixture which did precisely this: he became another ---, he became ----- ----. When he drank the potion again, he turned back into ----. He enjoyed changing into Hyde and doing whatever he wanted without being ----. He set up the laboratory for --- to live in, and ordered the servants to obey him. Things were tricky when Hyde was caught for trampling on the little girl and he had to pay compensation with a cheque written by Henry Jekyll. After this, Jekyll opened a bank account for ----. Two months before the murder of Carew, Jekyll found that he went to sleep as Jekyll but woke up as Hyde without taking the ----. After this, he decided not to take the potion but to be Jekyll all the time until one night he lost his ---- and took the potion; it had a very strong --- and he murdered Carew as a result. From then onwards, he decided ---- to become Hyde again. His dark side got the better of him and he did some bad things as ----. This caused him to ----- into Hyde without taking the potion: one morning in Regent's Park, he found that he had changed into Hyde. He didn't know what to do. He decided to ask Lanyon to fetch the drugs from his laboratory, and then visited Lanyon where he took the ---- and changed back into Jekyll. From that moment onwards, he has had to take more and more drugs just to stay as ----. Hyde was ---- over him. He knows that either he will be hung as the ----- of Carew, or he will manage to --- himself.

Comprehension questions

What was Jekyll's upbringing like? Why were the seeds of him becoming "Jekyll and Hyde" sown then?

What experiments did Jekyll pursue and why did other scientists like Lanyon regard him as misguided for doing them?

What are Jekyll's emotions when he tramples on the girl talked about in the first chapter?

What were the circumstances that led up to the murder of Carew?

What does Jekyll decide to do after the murder of Carew?

What evidence is there that Jekyll is being taken over by Hyde?

What happens in Regent's Park that shocks Jekyll so much?

What does Jekyll feel towards Hyde and what does Hyde feel towards Jekyll?

Analytical questions

What evidence is there that Jekyll is an "unreliable narrator"?

Why do you think Stevenson wrote this last section of the novel when the reader already knows the answer to the mystery?

How does Stevenson build up a sense of drama and horror in this section?

How does Stevenson build up sympathy for Jekyll and, to a lesser extent, Hyde?

Evaluative questions

How successful is this last section of the novel?

Creative response tasks

Write Hyde's diary for the events described in this novel, describing his feelings when he tramples upon the girl, when he has to pay compensation, when he meets Utterson, when he murders Carew, when he goes on his nightly adventures, and when he returns in Regent's Park and visits Lanyon. Describe his feelings towards Jekyll.

You can watch YouTube videos I made about this section here:
http://www.youtube.com/watch?v=G842fM-oxuU
http://www.youtube.com/watch?v=Tm9zkeIq-fE

POSSIBLE ANSWERS in brief & bold

Comprehension questions

What was Jekyll's upbringing like? Why were the seeds of him becoming "Jekyll and Hyde" sown then? **He always had two sides to his nature: he had a "gaiety of disposition", which meant in those days that he wanted to be sexually promiscuous with the opposite sex, but he always wanted to be respectable and an important, high status member of society. The two things were only possible if he hid his reckless, wild side from the general public. Thus we can see that he had a "duality" of nature: two sides, a side that wanted to "appear good", and a side that wanted to commit what was regarded then as "sinful" or "bad" acts.**

What experiments did Jekyll pursue and why did other scientists like Lanyon regard him as misguided for doing them? **He pursued "transcendental" or "mystical" experiments which attempted to separate the different sides of the human soul. He was regarded as being unscientific because what he was searching for was not viewed as a valid topic for scientific study.**

What are Jekyll's emotions when he tramples on the girl talked about in the first chapter? **He doesn't appear to really care about the girl at all and views the matter as a problem only because he was nearly lynched for being violent to her.**

What were the circumstances that led up to the murder of Carew? **Jekyll had not taken the drug from some time, vowing to give it up altogether, but when he did "give in" and take it again its strength was greatly increased because he hadn't taken it in a long while. This meant that its effect was much stronger and this, in turn, led to him murdering Carew without any reason at all.**

What does Jekyll decide to do after the murder of Carew? **He decides to give up taking the drug altogether**

What evidence is there that Jekyll is being taken over by Hyde? **Sometimes he would go to sleep as Henry Jekyll but then wake up as Mr Hyde.**

What happens in Regent's Park that shocks Jekyll so much? **He turns into Hyde suddenly during the day. He had not taken the drug. Hyde is wanted for murder and therefore is terrified of being caught and hung for the crime.**

What does Jekyll feel towards Hyde and what does Hyde feel towards Jekyll? **Jekyll feels "paternal" towards Hyde: he wants to indulge Hyde like a kind father might indulge a spoilt son. Hyde has nothing but contempt for Jekyll and would get rid of him if he weren't killing himself as well.**

Analytical questions

What evidence is there that Jekyll is an "unreliable narrator"? **Jekyll is a narrator who does not fully describe things that might make him uncomfortable. For example, he only makes very short** references to incidents that occupy a large part of the first part of the book: the trampling of the child, the murder of Carew and Lanyon's response to seeing Hyde turn into Jekyll are only briefly described. **He appears to "skim" over these details because he doesn't want to think about the implications of what he is done. He comes across as a very selfish and self-obsessed man who cares much more about not being caught and his own enjoyment than other people: he never expresses guilt for what he has done, only regret that things have turned out badly for him.**

Why do you think Stevenson wrote this last section of the novel when the reader already knows the answer to the mystery? **Stevenson aimed to write much more than a horror story: he wanted to write a story which was a "psychological fable about the human condition". This section attempts to show the workings of Jekyll's mind and reveals that far from being the opposite of Hyde, Jekyll always had "Hyde" hidden inside him. Behind the veneer of respectability lurked a monster.**

How does Stevenson build up a sense of drama and horror in this section? **The horror in this section is largely psychological. We feel horrified by the way in which Jekyll seems to love and care for Hyde, by the way in which he dismisses his crimes as unimportant and indeed at one point talks about how happy he felt when he was murdering Carew. Jekyll's self-pitying words are nauseating to read and make the reader angry that a man who had so much could enjoy becoming a psycho-path.**

How does Stevenson build up sympathy for Jekyll and, to a lesser extent, Hyde? **We feel sympathy for the way in which Jekyll becomes "corrupted" by the drug and the opportunities it offers to him. Even though he has confessed to enjoying murdering Carew, we can't help but feel a degree of sympathy for him when he talks about how degraded and humiliated he has become by his experiment. While we may hate Jekyll, we still see and, to a certain extent, feel his pain.**

Evaluative questions

How successful is this last section of the novel? **While the first half of the novel relied upon the classic tropes of the horror/mystery story to keep the reader interested, this last section maintains the reader's interest by getting us to think very carefully about Jekyll's state of mind and his perspective upon events we have already read about. Furthermore, this narrative "fills in the holes" of the narrative: we still don't quite know why Hyde had to demand Lanyon fetched the drugs from Jekyll's house. We realise now that Jekyll had turned into Hyde in Regent's Park and was desperate to change back to Jekyll but had no safe way of getting home. One of the chief pleasures in re-reading the** novel is thinking again and again about Jekyll's predicament, which is possibly a predicament of many of us: how can we do what we want and yet be accepted in the eyes of society? Often our desires are in conflict with what society expects from us. This last part of the narrative explores this issue and reveals that we are all in a tragic situation like Jekyll: our inner-most desires will, in the end, kill us.

Speaking and listening exercises to do on the novel

EXERCISE 1: Working in pairs, imagine you are a **psychiatrist** or **psychotherapist** or **counsellor** and you are **interviewing** various characters in the novel regarding their thoughts and feelings concerning the main events. You could interview:

Dr Jekyll: he could discuss his "duality of mind", his desire to appear respectable and yet indulge in "undignified pleasures", how the drug has got a grip on him, his fears about turning into Hyde, his love of Hyde etc., his reflections upon trampling upon the girl and murdering Carew.

Mr Hyde: he could discuss his love of pleasure, the sorts of things he likes doing, his hatred of Jekyll, his fear of being hung, his reflections upon trampling upon the girl, meeting Enfield, Utterson and Lanyon and murdering Carew

Mr Utterson: his shock regarding Jekyll and Hyde, how he discovered the truth about Jekyll, his worries for Jekyll throughout the novel.

Dr Lanyon: his shock at seeing Hyde turning into Jekyll, how all of his scientific ideas have been shattered now that he has seen this transformation.

Poole: his shock and concern at learning that his master was Hyde; his trauma regarding having to deal with Hyde for so long; his thoughts and feelings towards Jekyll.

EXERCISE 2: Put Jekyll and Hyde **on trial**. Set things up so that you have a prosecuting lawyer, who attacks Hyde and Jekyll for the murder of Carew and other crimes. Have a defence lawyer who tries to say that Jekyll was not in his right mind when he murdered Carew, he was Hyde. Call witnesses for prosecution and defence: these could be characters from the novel, but also could be police inspectors, psychotherapists, doctors etc.

EXERCISE 3: Hold a **chat show** a bit like Jeremy Kyle in which the main characters from the novel are invited to discuss what happened to them during the novel.

EXERCISE 4: Devise a series of **freeze-frames** for each chapter of the book which are pictures of the key moments in that chapter and include a narrator who explains what people in the freeze-frame are doing.

EXERCISE 5: Devise a **five minute drama** in groups of four in which you make use of a narrator and you show a very short version of the whole novel, boiling it down to its very basic actions, events and ideas. Use the chapter headings as your scenes, e.g. have a scene for 'Story of the Door' etc. You can also buy my script of the novel which includes a fully dramatized version of the play using the chapter headings.

Literary criticism of the novel

FIRST REVIEWS

The Times, 25th January 1885. Stevenson felt this positive review, published shortly after the book came out, helped make the book such a success:

> Nothing Mr. Stevenson has written as yet has so strongly impressed us with the versatility of his very original genius as this sparsely-printed little shilling volume...every connoisseur who reads the story once must certainly read it twice. He will read it the first time, passing from surprise to surprise, in a curiosity that keeps growing, because it is never satisfied...Never for a moment, in the most startling situations, has he lost his grasp of the ground-facts of a wonderful and supernatural problem.

Julia Wedgewood, *Contemporary Review*, April 1886 noted the lack of women in the story, an aspect which many critics have investigated since:

> Whereas most fiction deals with the relation between man and woman...the author of this strange tale takes an even narrower range, and sets himself to investigate the meaning of the word *self*. No woman's name occurs in the book, no romance is even suggested in it; it depends on the interest of an idea...

IS HYDE A RAPIST?

Gerald Manley Hopkins, *Letter to Robert Bridges*, October 28th 1886 noted that Hyde's crimes were probably too terrible to be written about in a novel:

> You are certainly wrong about Hyde being overdrawn: my Hyde is worse. The trampling scene is perhaps a convention: he was thinking of something unsuitable for fiction...Stevenson is master of a consummate style and each phase is finished as in poetry.

THE ORIGINALITY OF THE STORY
C. K Chesterton, *The Real Stab of the Story*, 1927

Chesterton believed that although Stevenson says the story is set in London, it felt it was "unmistakeably" taking place in Edinburgh, Stevenson's native city in Scotland. He felt that Utterson behaved like a Scottish lawyer, and that Jekyll's two-faced nature was "Caledonian" or Scottish, appearing to behave like a Scottish Puritan. Chesterton wrote:

> The real stab of the story is not in the discovery that the one man is two men; but in the discovery that the two men are one man...The point of the story is not that a man *can* cut himself off from his conscience, but that he cannot.

Chesterton was one of the first critics to notice the originality in this idea, and to explore the ways in which the novel is different from many other horror novels in that it is "psychological" in its structure and theme.

THE THREE PERSONALITIES

Vladimir Nabokov in *A Phenomenon of Style* made three major points about the book:

> First, he felt that Jekyll was not a good man, but a "composite" character, a "mixture of good and bad"... Nabokov sees him as a hypocrite who hides his sins from other people. He is "vindictive, never forgiving Lanyon with whom he disagrees in scientific matters... Nabokov felt that Hyde was "mingled with him, within him. Into this mixture of good and bad in Dr. Jekyll, the bad can be separated as Hyde, who is a precipitate of pure evil..."

> Second, Nabokov believed that Jekyll is not really changed into Hyde but "projects" his evil side which becomes Hyde.

> Third, Nabokov believed that there were three personalities: Jekyll, Hyde and a "third, the Jekyll residue when Hyde takes over...Hyde still wants to change back to Jekyll. This is the significant point". For Nabokov this indicated that Jekyll still lives inside Hyde and is with Hyde when he is doing his evil.

Nabokov points out that Stevenson makes his story believable and realistic by having it observed by "matter-of-fact" persons, Utterson and Enfield, while Lanyon was used so that he could notice as a scientist all the details about the transformation. Nabokov noted like a number of other critics such as Elaine Showalter in her book *Sexual Anarchy: Gender and Culture at the Fin de Siecle* that the all-male atmosphere of the book, and the fact that Hyde is Jekyll's "benefactor" and "protégée" suggest that Jekyll was homosexual and liked to have homosexual adventures in London.

THE USE OF PRONOUNS

Peter Garrett in *Instabilities of Meaning, Morality and Narration*, from Cries and Voices: Reading *Jekyll and Hyde, Dr Jekyll and Mr Hyde after One Hundred Years* pp. 59-72

Garrett points out that the story constantly uses different pronouns when Jekyll and other characters talk about Hyde: sometimes Jekyll talks about Hyde in the first person, using "I", and, at other times, he calls him "he" or in some cases "it". Garrett points out that in his account, Jekyll often refuses to identify with Hyde by talking about Hyde's "infamy", but then at other times, Jekyll identifies with Hyde's feelings as in the passage when he describes murdering Carew: "With a transport of glee, I mauled the unresisting body, tasting delight from every blow." Sometimes, Garrett points out that there is an "unnamed narrator" telling Jekyll's account as in the sentence: "Between these two I now felt I had to choose", either the "I" of the narration has to choose between Jekyll and Hyde, and yet this is odd because it is Jekyll who is supposed to be narrating. Garrett asks who this "anonymous" narrator is. Garrett points out that Jekyll problem is the same as anyone who tells their story because they separate the "I" on the page from their actual self who is writing the story. Garrett goes on to show that after talking about Hyde in the first person at the very end of the narrative, Jekyll "reasserts his separation from Hyde" when he writes: "Will Hyde die on the scaffold?"

Garrett talks a great deal about the "instability" of who Jekyll is: he is not two people, but many, and we, the readers, and the other characters are constantly searching for an answer to this question. Ultimately, the quest for finding out who Jekyll is leads to Utterson and Poole breaking down the door in an act of violence which leads to Jekyll's suicide. Garrett notes that Jekyll's last words are spoken in the 'The Last Night': "Utterson for God's sake have mercy!" Again, we wonder who is speaking here. Is it Jekyll? Is it Hyde who is speaking with Jekyll's voice? Is it Jekyll speaking with Hyde's voice? Did Jekyll turn into Hyde when he killed himself, or did Hyde reply and then kill himself? There are no answers to these questions, and that's why the story remains a mystery after many readings.

HYDE AND EVOLUTION

Patrick Brantlinger, *An Unconscious Allegory about the Masses and Mass Literacy*

The critic Brantlinger examined in this essay the circumstances of the publication of the novel. She points out that Stevenson always had mixed feelings about the success of Dr. Jekyll, calling it a "Gothic gnome" and a "fine bogey tale". She shows that Stevenson's wife made him turn the story into a "moral allegory", i.e. a story that has a particular moral, or message in which Jekyll is effectively punished for his sins. Brantlinger shows that many critics have argued that the tale is an "allegory" about good and evil, but she argues that the novel be read as an allegory about "the emergence of a mass consumer society in the late-Victorian period." She argues that the murder of Sir Danvers Carew has some similarities with the real-life murders of the 1882 Phoenix Park murders in Dublin in which Irish nationalists murdered a respectable English gentleman. She argues that many readers of the time may have seen Hyde as being like an "Irish Fenian" or nationalist: most of these traits – his violence, his hairy arms, his short stature – were recognisably "working class" and possibly "Irish" for middle-class Victorian readers. He fits the stereotype of the criminal drawn up by the criminologist Cesar Lombroso in 1886, when he described criminals as having certain physical traits such as being ugly and deformed in their looks. She shows that one of Hyde's few "upper class" traits is his hand-writing and this is what makes him cause so much chaos and enables him to survive: he can write notes that enable him to get drugs, write cheques to pay off people who are unhappy with him, and write swear words all over Jekyll's sacred texts. Although Stevenson deliberately takes out all references to the contemporary society he was writing about such as the problem of the Irish/a criminal working class, for Brantlinger Hyde represents these worries and anxieties of upper-class Victorian society: he is a symbol of the destructiveness of the "lower orders".

THE "HYDING" OF CRIMES
Katherine Linehan, Sex, Secrecy and *Self-Alienation in Strange Case of Dr. Jekyll and Mr Hyde*

Lineham points out how Hyde is "closer than a wife" to Jekyll at the end of the book. She views Hyde as an "expression of underground sexual appetite on Jekyll's part" and discusses how critics have viewed Hyde's violence with some critics arguing that Hyde's shows "heterosexual sadism" while others like Nabokov and Showalter try to show that Hyde's acts suggest forbidden homosexual practices. Linehan points out that Stevenson openly rebelled against his Puritan upbringing which labelled sex as sinful. She refers to a letter of Stevenson's which vents his anger about Hyde being viewed as someone who is sinful because of his sexual appetite; as a result Stevenson thought that people failed to see that Hyde's cruelty comes not from his desire to have sex, but from Jekyll's desire to hide everything he did. Stevenson was angry because people mistake sexuality for evil, whereas it was actually hypocrisy that caused evil. Lineham develops a long and complex argument in her essay that essentially shows that it is the loss of Jekyll's "soul" which is the crime and that it happens because Jekyll is intoxicated with the way in which he can hide his actions by becoming Hyde. We see this in the 'Full Statement of the Case' because initially Hyde does not commit terrible crimes, but comes to become progressively worse because he realises that he can get away with it. Jekyll becomes obsessed by his disguise; this is what leads him astray and enables Hyde to grow in power and strength as the story progresses.

Writing essays on the novel, including exam responses

Here is a GSCE question on the novel, based on an extract. This is the extract, which is the opening of 'The Carew Murder Case':

Nearly a year later, in the month of October, 18—, London was startled by a crime of singular ferocity and rendered all the more notable by the high position of the victim. The details were few and startling. A maid servant living alone in a house not far from the river had gone upstairs to bed about eleven. Although a fog rolled over the city in the small hours, the early part of the night was cloudless, and the lane, which the maid's window overlooked, was brilliantly lit by the full moon. It seems she was romantically given, for she sat down upon her box, which stood immediately under the window, and fell into a dream of musing (she used to say, with streaming tears, when she narrated that experience), never had she felt more at peace with all men or thought more kindly of the world. And as she so sat she became aware of an aged beautiful gentleman with white hair, drawing near along the lane; and advancing to meet him, another and very small gentleman, to whom at first she paid less attention. When they had come within speech (which was just under the maid's eyes) the older man bowed and accosted the other with a very pretty manner of politeness. It did not seem as if the subject of his address were of great importance; indeed, from his pointing, it sometimes appeared as if he were only inquiring his way; but the moon shone on his face as he spoke, and the girl was pleased to watch it, it seemed to breathe such an innocent and old-world kindness of disposition, yet with something high too, as of a well-founded self-content. Presently her eye wandered to the other, and she was surprised to recognise in him a certain Mr. Hyde, who had once visited her master and for whom she had conceived a dislike. He had in his hand a heavy cane, with which he was trifling; but he answered never a word, and seemed to listen with an ill-contained impatience. And then all of a sudden he broke out in a great flame of anger, stamping with his foot, brandishing the cane, and carrying on (as the maid described it) like a madman. The old gentleman took a step back, with the air of one very much surprised and a trifle hurt; and at that Mr. Hyde broke out of all bounds and clubbed him to the earth. And next moment, with ape-like fury, he was trampling his victim under foot and hailing down a storm of blows, under which the bones were audibly shattered and the body jumped upon the roadway. At the horror of these sights and sounds, the maid fainted.

GCSE QUESTION

How does Stevenson's writing here make this moment in the novel so horrifying?

Remember to support your ideas with details from the extract.

What do you think of the following response and how do you think it could be improved? Re-write it, correcting any mistakes you spot, and adding detail where you think is necessary.

STUDENT RESPONSE

I fink this writing passage shows that Mr Hyde is a horrible bloke. I have a few reasons for showing this. First, you have to got to fink about wot happened before this scene happened, this is chapter 4 of the book, and so you realise that the writer has built up to this moment. We already don't like Mr Hyde because we have seen him trample on a young girl of eight and make Henry Jekyll really unhappy. He already seems to be a dodgy geezer. So that meanz you're on the edge of your seat before the scene begins; you know something dodgy is gonna happen the moment Hyde appearz. That's important coz when the maid sees Mr Hyde carrying the "heavy cane" you fink, uh-oh wots gonna happen now, Mr Hyde is gonna do somefing real bad.

But wots horrifying is that the violence he commits is far worse than anything he has done before. Stevenson makes the scene horrifying by describing the scene in such detail. He uses a metaphor "great flame of anger" to suggest that Hyde is burning with anger; this makes you fink Hyde is like a great big bonfire full of hatred and anger. Then he uses a Similie to say that Hyde is like "a madman", this makes me fink Hyde is a syko who dosent care wot anyone finks of him. Wot makes it even worse is that the old geezer wot he tramples on and beats to death is very nice, he shows "a very pretty manner of politeness", in other words, he's very nice and polite to Hyde, and wot does Hyde do him but beats him to death? This is horrifying because it makes you realise that Hyde is a rite proper syko:

> The old gentleman took a step back, with the air of one very much surprised and a trifle hurt; and at that Mr. Hyde broke out of all bounds and clubbed him to the earth. And next moment, with ape-like fury, he was trampling his victim under foot and hailing down a storm of blows, under which the bones were audibly shattered and the body jumped upon the roadway.

This quote shows he is a rite proper syko. Don't you think? He is described as having "ape-like fury", this makes me fink that Hyde is like an animal who is less evolved than a human being. Then the description of the bones being "audibly shattered" make you hear the crunching of the bones of the poor old gentleman: this imagery makes you think of how painful the old man's death must be. You can see it clearly too because Stevenson uses visual imagery when he says there was a "storm of blows": this metaphor suggests that he hit the old man very quickly in the same way rain falls in a storm. Then, there's more horror when he is described as "jumping" on the old man. You know that the scene must have been terrifying coz the maid is described as "fainting". Overall, you see that Stevenson has made the scene horrifying by using a number of different techniques. 1. He has structured the story so that we're already worried about wot Hyde mite do 2. He has used some well good imagery to make us see the murder in very clear detail.

Oh and I almost 4got, the setting is described in a creepy way and this is somefing wot adds to the suspense coz it's a foggy, cloudless night wiv the full moon shinning. Spooky or wot? It's like there mite be wherewolves or somefing.

How you might improve this response:

First, this candidate needs to improve their spelling and grammar. Spelling mistakes such as "fink", "4got" and slang expressions such as "gonna" are not going to get you a top grade. Furthermore, the candidate is very repetitious: he repeats words like "described" far too much. He needs to find synonyms to describe this words.

Second, there are many good points in the essay that need to be further developed and re-phrased. The candidate makes a good point in the first paragraph by pointing out how Stevenson has "structured" the novel so that we're already in suspense BEFORE the chapter begins. He shows that he knows what has happened previously by referring to incidents that are quite frightening in the book. However, he could have discussed the structure of this particular passage as well; he could have talked about how the scene begins in a very peaceful fashion, with the street being quiet and the old man greeting Hyde in a polite fashion, and then ends with a terrible murder. Stevenson builds up a sense of horror by painting a vivid picture of a very nice old man being savagely murdered. He does this very "economically", that is he quickly sketches a picture of the old man being very pleasant: he is a "beautiful aged gentleman" who "bows" before Hyde. This accentuates the horror because it is a good and defenceless man who has been murdered.

Third, there are a number of good points about how the imagery of the passage adds to the horror. However, at one point, the candidate just copies out a large chunk of the passage and repeats a previous point, without analysing the passage in any depth. This is a common mistake of weaker answers, they tend to copy out passages and not really analyse them. To give the candidate credit, he does pick out some phrases which are relevant and analyse them: "great flame of anger", "audibly shattered", "ape-like fury", and "storm of blows" are all good phrases to analyse and by and large the candidate does tackle them in a reasonably analytical fashion, except that his expression can be too informal at times. Here we see him "integrating" the quotes into his answer, and talking about the effect of the quotations. He could have gone into more depth though, by discussing in more detail what the imagery makes the reader see, think and feel.

Fourth, the candidate could have looked in more depth at the characterisations, and shown how the writer builds up a sense of horror by slowly revealing the true depths of Hyde's evil. We also feel a deeper sense of unease because of Hyde's connection with Jekyll.

Fifth, the candidate could have examined Stevenson's use of punctuation to build up a sense of horror. There are a number of sentences you could analyse in depth but this one is good for examining to see the effect of the punctuation:

> And then all of a sudden he broke out in a great flame of anger, stamping with his foot, brandishing the cane, and carrying on (as the maid described it) like a madman.

Notice how Stevenson builds up a sense of horror by listing the various horrific events that happen and separating them off with commas: we have first of the "flame of anger" which describes Hyde's emotions, then the stamping of his foot which suggests the rage he feels and conveys the noises he is making, then we see him "brandishing his cane" and then finally, at the very end of the sentence the devastating simile that he is carrying on "like a madman". The commas enable the writer to build up a terrifying picture of Hyde's feelings, what he is physically doing and his psychotic demeanour.

Here is another question, which is a straight "essay" question rather than one that requires you to analyse a passage. Personally, I think it is a better question to respond to because it allows a good candidate to show more knowledge of the novel than the other question.

How far are you able to feel sympathy for Dr Jekyll? Remember to support your ideas with details from the novel.

To pen a good answer to this question, you will need to structure your answer carefully. First, you need to brainstorm all your thoughts in response to the question, using the **5Ws + H (What, where, when, who, why, how)** to help you:

When do we feel sympathy for Jekyll? **When** do we not feel sympathy for him?

What makes us feel sympathy towards him? What techniques does Stevenson use to make us feel sympathetic towards him?

Where in the novel are the moments in the novel that make us feel sympathetic towards him?

Who feels sympathy for him in the book and how does this affect our feelings towards him?

How does Stevenson makes us feel sympathy for him?

KEY POINTS

Stevenson **structures** the novel carefully so that there is a great deal of mystery about Dr Jekyll. While we may feel sympathy for him at certain points in the novel, this isn't the primary reason why we keep turning the pages: the central cause for our interest is the mystery. However, along the way, we feel sympathy, to a degree, that Jekyll has become "mixed up" with Mr Hyde: this is before we know the truth about who Hyde is. So, for example, there are key moments such as 'The Incident at the Window' when we see Jekyll looking so unhappy, when he shows he is full of "abject terror" that make us feel pity for him. But by the time of Jekyll's confession, which is the last section of the book, we have lost sympathy for him: he has conducted a dangerous experiment which has led to the abuse of many people and the murder of Carew. Even so, towards the end of the confession, we feel sympathy once again when he turns back into Mr Hyde in Regent's Park: Jekyll has determined to live a life without Hyde, but has failed and now is a hunted and humiliated man. Jekyll behaves like a drug addict, desperate for the drug to turn him back into Jekyll.

Stevenson's **characterisation** of Jekyll is complex: as the novel progresses he is revealed as a complicated man with contradictory desires and aspirations. This evinces a degree of sympathy because, in this sense, Jekyll is like all of us: we are all complicated and if we had discovered an "ebullition" like the one he finds, we may well have enjoyed being "Hyde" for a while. Thus we can see that Stevenson creates sympathy for Jekyll by describing his "duality of nature", by exploring how he always had "two sides" to him: the side that wanted to appear respectable and have people's admiration, and the side that wanted to act on his deepest desires. However, we are torn in our sympathies because it becomes clear that rather than Hyde being a "different person" created by the drug is actually a manifestation of Jekyll's innermost desires. This is clearly seen when Jekyll describes the murder of Carew:

> Instantly the spirit of hell awoke in me and raged. With a transport of glee, I mauled the unresisting body, tasting delight from every blow; and it was not till weariness had begun to succeed, that I was suddenly, in the top fit of my delirium, struck through the heart by a cold thrill of terror

The **pronoun** "I" is important here because Jekyll is actually Hyde when he murders Carew and has been describing what Hyde does in the third person at certain points, but here we see him using the first person. This indicates that it is actually Jekyll who is killing Carew and that Hyde is a "smoke-screen" for the dark side of Jekyll. Stevenson's writing here is full of energy and while we don't feel sympathy for Jekyll, we certainly are both fascinated and horrified to read the description of a murder: we see that Jekyll feels a "transport of glee", in other words he is ecstatically happy when he kills Carew, he feels "delight from every blow": this is a man who revels and enjoys violence, and only stops being violent when he is tired.

Stevenson uses a great deal of **emotive language** to evoke sympathy for Jekyll. This whole novel is an anatomy of the changing feelings of Jekyll: we see him exhibit a whole multiplicity of moods and "dispositions": he moves from feeling extreme joy or ecstasy, to feeling suicidally depressed.

Sequencing exercise

Learning objectives: to learn how Stevenson develops a sense of horror in his narrative through his use of description.

TASK 1: Read the quotes and then put the quotes in the order that they occur in the book, matching them with the correct chapter heading.

TASK 2: Order the quotes with the most horrifying first, and least horrifying last. Discuss and make notes upon WHY you have sequenced them in this way.

The extracts are taken from these chapters but not in this order:

Chapter 1 'Story of the Door'; Chapter 2, 'Search for Mr Hyde'; Chapter 4, 'The Carew Murder Case'; Chapter 7, 'Incident at the Window'; Chapter 8, 'The Last Night'; Chapter 9 'Dr Lanyon's Narrative'; Chapter 10, 'Dr Jekyll's Full Statement of the Case'.

QUOTE 1: Right in the midst there lay the body of a man sorely contorted and still twitching. They drew near on tiptoe, turned it on its back and beheld the face of Edward Hyde.

QUOTE 2: I knew myself, at the first breath of this new life, to be more wicked, tenfold more wicked, sold a slave to my original evil; and the thought, in that moment, braced and delighted me like wine.

QUOTE 3: But the hand which I now saw, clearly enough, in the yellow light of a mid-London morning, lying half shut on the bed-clothes, was lean, corded, knuckly, of a dusky pallor and thickly shaded with a swart growth of hair. It was the hand of Edward Hyde.

QUOTE 4: Instantly the spirit of hell awoke in me and raged. With a transport of glee, I mauled the unresisting body, tasting delight from every blow;

QUOTE 5: His face became suddenly black and the features seemed to melt and alter – and the next moment, I had sprung to my feet and leaped back against the wall, my arm raised to shield me from that prodigy, my mind submerged in terror.

QUOTE 6: The pleasures which I made haste to seek in my disguise were, as I have said, undignified; I would scarce use a harder term. But in the hands of Edward Hyde, they soon began to turn toward the monstrous.

QUOTE 7: Well, sir, the two ran into one another naturally enough at the corner; and then came the horrible part of the thing; for the man trampled calmly over the child's body and left her screaming on the ground.

QUOTE 8: My life is shaken to its roots; sleep has left me; the deadliest terror sits by me at all hours of the day and night

QUOTE 9: Mr Hyde was pale and dwarfish, he gave an impression of deformity without any nameable malformation, he had a displeasing smile...

QUOTE 10: And then all of a sudden he broke out in a great flame of anger, stamping with his foot, brandishing the cane, and carrying on (as the maid described it) like a madman.

QUOTE 11: 'That is just what I was about to venture to propose,' returned the doctor with a smile. But the words were hardly uttered, before the smile was struck out of his face and succeeded by an expression of such abject terror and despair, as froze the very blood of the two gentlemen below.

Answers to sequencing exercise

Quote 1: from 'The Last Night'
Quote 2: from 'Dr Jekyll's Full Statement of the Case'
Quote 3: from 'Dr Jekyll's Full Statement of the Case'
Quote 4: from 'Dr Jekyll's Full Statement of the Case'
Quote 5: from 'Dr Lanyon's Narrative'
Quote 6: from 'Dr Jekyll's Full Statement of the Case'
Quote 7: from 'The Story of the Door'
Quote 8: from 'Dr Lanyon's Narrative'
Quote 9: from 'The Search for Mr Hyde'
Quote 10: from 'The Carew Murder Case'
Quote 11: from 'Incident at the Window'

Answers to fill-in-the-blanks summary exercises

1 Story of the Door – fill-in-the-gaps answers: Trouble; door; trample on; girl; £100; Henry Jekyll; respectable; genuine; blackmailed
2 Search for Mr Hyde – fill-in-the-gaps answers: Will; Edward Hyde; fallen out; face; address; key; obey

3 **Dr Jekyll was Quite at Ease** – fill-in-the-gaps answers: **Dinner; trusted; blackmailed; Mr Hyde; disappears** or **dies.**
4 **The Carew Murder Case** – fill-in-the-gaps answers: **Death; breaks; Mr Utterson; clients; Henry Jekyll's; broken stick; cheque-book; bank; seen**
5 **Incident of the Letter** – fill-in-the-gaps answers: **deathly ill; Hyde; escaped; unworthy; letter; hand-writing; forge**
6 **Remarkable Incident of Dr Lanyon** – fill-in-the-gaps answers: **Found; good Lanyon** and **Utterson; anybody; die; dead; complain; punishment; after; refuses**
7 **Incident at the Window** – fill-in-the-gaps answers: **Open; Jekyll's; depressed; walk; terror; silence.**
8 **The Last Night** -- fill-in-the-gaps answers: **"foul play"; hallway; strange; "made away with"; ill; smaller; "have mercy!"; dressed; killed; Jekyll; Utterson's; Lanyon's; "confession"**
9 **Dr Lanyon's Narrative** -- fill-in-the-gaps answers **Drawer; drawer; midnight; watch; Satan; Jekyll; Hyde; murdered; "The deadliest terror"**
10 **Henry Jekyll's Full Statement of the Case** -- fill-in-the-gaps answers: **good** and the **bad; person; Edward Hyde; Jekyll; caught; Hyde; Hyde; potion; self-control; effect; Jekyll; change; drugs; Jekyll; taking; murderer; kill**

Glossary

conventional morality – the ordinary rules of everyday life, the code of behaviour that 'normal' people abide by
dualistic -- dualism - the doctrine that reality consists of two basic opposing elements, often taken to be mind and matter (or mind and body), or good and evil
inarticulacy – being unable to express something in words
extraneous – irrelevant, not needed
hysteric – a person who reacts in a hysterical manner to life, making a great deal of fuss about nothing!
irreverent – not being respectful, disrespectful
malevolence – badness, nastiness, evil
motif – repeated idea
neurotic – a person who is obsessively and needlessly worried
perturbed – upset, disturbed
proto-existentialist – the forerunner of an existentialist, who were people believed that one should do what you want, follow your unconscious desires, rather than being constrained by

conventional morality – a set of rules which enable you to live what society deems to be a good life.

repressed – holding back, keeping back your emotions

repression – see above

resonances -- associations

social position – your place in society

subconscious – another word for the 'unconscious'

the unconscious – the place in the human mind where one's repressed desires are kept

undiscriminating – not very picky, not being able to make good decisions about things and people

Select bibliography

Chesterton, C., 2001. *Robert Louis Stevenson*. New edition based on a much older book ed. London: House of Stratus.

Daiches, D., 1973. *Robert Louis Stevenson and His World*. London: Pictorial Biography.

Gray, W., 2004. *Robert Louis Stevenson -- A Literary Life*. Great Britain: Palgrave Macmillan.

Harman, C., 2006. *Robert Louis Stevenson -- A Biography*. Harper Perennial ed. London: Harper .

Linehan, E. b. K., 2003. *Strange Case of Dr. Jekyll and Mr Hyde -- A Norton Critical Edition*. New York: W.W. Norton.

Luckhurst, R., 2006. *Strange Case of Dr Jekyll and Mr Hyde and Other Tales*. Oxford World Classics ed. Oxford: Oxford University Press.

Mighall, E. b. R., 2003. *The Strange Case of Dr Jekyll and Mr Hyde and other tales of terror*. London: Penguin Classics.

THE END

CPSIA information can be obtained at www.ICGtesting.com
Printed in the USA
LVOW07s2030231015

459506LV00042B/2493/P